MY TIME AT BAT
A STORY OF PERSEVERANCE

Chuck Hinton

An imprint of Pneuma Life Publishing
Largo, MD

Copyright © 2002 Charles E. Hinton, Jr.

Christian Living Books, Inc.
An imprint of Pneuma Life Publishing
P. O. Box 7584
Largo, MD 20792
301-218-9092
www.ChristianLivingBooks.com

All rights reserved under the international copyright law. No part of this book may be reproduced or transmitted in any form or by any means, electronic or mechanical, including photocopying, recording, or by any information storage and retrieval system, without the express, written permission of the publisher.

Printed in the United States of America

Hardback ISBN 1-56229-003-7
Paperback ISBN 1-56229-176-9

Library of Congress Control Number: 2002106289

Unless otherwise indicated, all Scripture quotations are taken from the King James Version of the Bible.

Dedication

This book is dedicated to the memory of my flower. We will surely miss her on a regular basis. It is going to take time to heal. Nevertheless, like other things, we shall overcome it. We will cherish the time that we shared with her. She was a most giving and loving person with a beautiful smile that she shared with everyone she met. I truly believe that she never met a stranger. She was always pleasant and kind to everyone.

Jonquil Hinton Hawkins (Joni)
December 9, 1960 – January 8, 2002

Contents

Foreword	vii
Preface	ix
Acknowledgments	xi
Chapter 1 • A Dream Come True	1
Chapter 2 • How It All Began	5
Chapter 3 • Following My Dream	17
Chapter 4 • The Minor Leagues	21
Chapter 5 • The High Life	29
Chapter 6 • The Expansion Washington Senators	37
Chapter 7 • On Stage at the Show	43
Chapter 8 • Many Years to Come	57
Chapter 9 • More Memorable Moments	69
Chapter 10 • An Inside-the-Park Look	81
Chapter 11 • Baseball in Black and White	89
Chapter 12 • Life After Baseball	93
Chapter 13 • Baseball Today	105
Chapter 14 • For Love of the Game	111
Epilogue	129

Foreword

A first time author, Chuck Hinton, displays an immense capacity for recall in detailing a life of eleven years of baseball in this book. However, after one reads to the story-line, one recognizes that within the baseball text is a revelation of moral fiber that is every bit as interesting as the work itself.

My Time At Bat–A Story of Perseverance clearly demonstrates that Chuck Hinton is a family man—one who does his baseball thing as a sideline. The reader finds this to be true from the opening paragraphs. He begins with a moving eulogy to his oldest daughter, Jonquil, who died only months before publication of these memoirs.

There's an adorable photograph of Chuck with his son, an athlete in high school.

His second of three daughters, Kimberly, was embraced in hour-after-hour of patient explanation of the intricacies of the game so that she could assist her father in writing the story of his life and career. And third and youngest daughter, Tiffany, reaped the portrayal of a father who had the pride of a king when she came home September 1, 2001 to be married.

In essence, *My Time At Bat–A Story of Perseverance* is an interesting read for fans of baseball, and an emotional time for those who have adoring families.

–Sam Lacy, BBWA
Hall of Fame '97

Preface

When I retired from Howard University and the D.C. Department of Recreation, I was given three retirement parties—the last of which was held at RFK Stadium. To my surprise, my daughter Kim had put together a small book that told a lot about me and my career. We passed it out as a memento to the attendees of what they called "Chuck's Roast." That was the start of this book.

Kim, who is in the publishing business, suggested I add to that memento and put together a larger book that fans and players would be proud to read and share. Therefore, I compiled memories that are dear to me. I hope the resulting book will be pleasing to read.

I found it easy to stay away from knocking players or other people. I don't want to do something that would damage someone. Sometimes you have to get things in the right perspective. You are competing against other teams, but you don't have to be unkind. Nor will you find any curse words in this book. I will not tell you what went on in the clubhouses with the players kidding each other or stealing signals or really working hard to break up a double play that could win a game but could put a player out for an entire career. There are many things I fail to talk about because I feel they need to stay among Major League players only.

What you will find is an encouraging story about what it was like to make it in the big league, complete with behind-the-scenes information and many funny stories. I want most of all to help others do some of the things that worked for me. What a life I have led, eleven years in the Major League.

I like to think this book will serve the baseball world a little differently in many ways from other books. I truly hope you will enjoy reading this book as much as I enjoyed putting it together.

Acknowledgments

Bunny, thank you for being there for me; for as long as I live, I will always be there for you. God's best to you.

I also would like to thank my family, as well as each of my former teammates and the players against whom I competed. I like to think I made many fans happy, for you all are the ones who made me give my best day in and day out.

I would like to give Kim credit for making this book a reality with all the information I remember and have put together. She was a daily reminder of what had to be done, that I should sit down and really think about what it was like and what it really meant to me. She cracked the whip often. However, she was kind and polite, and I truly thank her. When you have done something, as I have played Major League Baseball, you don't want to brag or always remind people that you did it. She simply told me that many people would like to know inside information and what it was like to be there. That is what I tried to do–give everyone a feeling of being there and make it simple so almost anyone could understand it.

No book is worth its weight unless it can put the reader into the writer's head or heart. Baseball was so much fun to me, and my love for the game and all that it stood for was a great thrill that I can't really put into words. If I could have, I would have paid baseball to play–but baseball paid me to have so much fun on the field against the best players in the world.

Just think–the best players in the world. I, Chuck Hinton, was one of them for eleven years, from 1961-1971. God has been so good to me in giving me the talent. My wife was always there for me, and I will be grateful to her always. I thank the many teams for their support. The fans–both home and away–were great, and they gave me a lot of encouragement.

My opponents gave me many reasons to want to excel because so many times they pushed me to be a real competitor. However, my Kim did everything to get these things into book form. For all the pushing and kind words to her Daddy, I truly thank her. My love will forever be hers.

Chapter One

A Dream Come True

Most people think you can sit and wait for success to come. I had to go after it. I put my talent on the line where the odds were greatly stacked against me—in Major League Baseball. I learned to keep myself in position to do what I had to do, to stay in shape, to keep my mind in the game, and to know how to win the battle with the pitcher, as a hitter and a base stealer.

It was not easy. The road from Rocky Mount, North Carolina, to the Major League was long and sometimes bumpy. There were times when I didn't know I would get there. So many hurdles were in my path, and there were always tests that I had to pass. But I was so raw and ready to show what I could do.

Growing up, I had always thought that if you could hit, run, catch and throw, you would make it in baseball. Boy, did I have a lot to learn! These things are all important—in most cases, a must—but they are only a part of what it takes to survive in the Minor Leagues, not to mention the Major Leagues. I didn't know just how much it took to be the kind of player I was required to be.

My Time at Bat — A Story of Perseverance

WHAT IT TAKES

Just about every kid dreams of becoming a professional athlete in most major sports. Little does he know what it takes to get the chance and then pass the test. When you are in your hometown playing a sport, you very well may be the best player there. But when you sign and go away to seek bigger opportunities, you may be the worst player there. What really separates the good from the average is doing what you do when it counts. Performing in clutch situations is not something just anyone can do. Knowing what you can do is so important. But knowing what to do, at all times, is even more important.

You have to study and retain so much information to play among the best. You can never make the same mistake twice. You listen to learn what will help you. And those things that will not do you any good you let fall by the wayside. You have to learn to respect those who are in charge, and, of course, you learn from those who have been there for years. Knowing when to talk is important. I think that being an all-around nice person is also important to be successful. You can't be everyone's friend, but you can be nice to everyone.

You learn early on that winning is the key. You learn that you have to be ready on defense on every pitch. Being in the right place at the right time is a must. You learn to think ahead about what to do and where to be in every situation. In other words, you must be able to think about the next play even before it happens. This is also true when you are at bat. You might think that facing the best pitchers in the world is an easy test. Well, let me tell you that in most cases, the pitcher has the advantage. The other team has discussed you ahead of time, and the pitcher of the day sometimes kept the chart the day before, recording what pitches were thrown to you and where, and what you did against those pitchers.

Then the pitcher goes over that information and plans his attack against you. If there is a weakness, he and his team will know and plan to pitch you and play you a certain way. There is nothing left to chance at the Major League level. In my years of hitting against all clubs, no matter what you did against them, they tended to stay with their play against you.

A Dream Come True

To hit effectively in the Major Leagues, you have to do some homework also. You, too, have to record what the other team does in certain situations. You have to know just what and where that next pitch will be. It's not luck that you know this. Looking for a certain pitch in a certain spot is what you live for because the hitter doesn't often miss that pitch.

One pitch a hitter usually could expect is a fastball when the pitcher was behind in the count one ball, no strikes; two balls, no strikes; three balls, one strike; sometimes even no balls, no strikes. It's called a cripple pitch. You don't want to miss those pitches because when the count is turned around and in the pitcher's favor, you are at his mercy, and believe me, it's not good. Your eyes are your best friend because you must see where the pitch is and if it is "hitable". That means that if you can't get a good swing and put the bat on the ball, then you have to pass that pitch up–that is, if you don't have two strikes against you.

At bat, you learn to concentrate to the point where you don't hear or see anyone but the pitcher you are facing.

Whether at bat or in the field, the physical part of baseball was easy. The mental part is what makes the difference. Talent will get you in the door, but mental toughness will keep you there.

Much of what you have to know in professional baseball you learn in the Minor League. After all, that's what the Minors are for. However, things are different in the Major League. In the Majors, you know what to do and how to get it done. You are there because you have earned that right. But to stay there, you must contribute day in and day out to the success of your team. It is not easy, by any means. You must learn from your mistakes. You must fight to keep any edge you can get. Every day, you have to be ready to play–and that means mentally as well as physically.

Besides *having* to earn your keep every day, you *should* do it for your fans. I always thought the fans deserved to see my best. No, it didn't put any added pressure on me; it was mainly my way of not letting myself get in any position but the best. To me, the fans were the reason we did what we did, and they paid to see us do it, so they deserved to see our best.

As a professional baseball player, how you handle yourself off the field is also very important. A team likes to have players it can depend on, on and off the field, because the team has so much invested in them. It is no secret

MY TIME AT BAT — A STORY OF PERSEVERANCE

that your team watches most of the things you do, good or bad. Adjustments have to be made all the time. There are many things you might not like, but for the best interest of you and the team, you make the necessary changes.

Life is about making adjustments. There are many times when you would like to do the things you are comfortable doing, but, because of others, you do what you have to do to keep peace or make the whole picture better. The adjustments off the field are much harder to deal with than playing in the Major League. Doing the best you can is all you can do. Make sure you have made the best decision, whatever the situation might be. This is part of being a complete person–which is as important as being a good player.

In the pages ahead, I will show you how I surpassed the hurdles, how I passed the tests, how I persevered along my journey to success in the Major Leagues–and in life. I hope my story and the principles I live by will help people, male or female, in all walks of life. I want most of all to tell you how it truly felt to be a Major Leaguer. It was a dream come true.

Chapter Two

How it All Began

I was born Charlie Edward Hinton Jr. to Charlie and Ada Hinton on May 3, 1934, in Rocky Mount, North Carolina. I was the second son of seven children–Doris, Charlie Leonard, Ellen, Ruth, myself, James "Checo" and Herman "Patches." I had quite a time living. As a baby, I had double pneumonia, and my parents didn't think I would survive. The first-born son in our family, Charlie Leonard, lived three months and twenty days, and then died of double pneumonia. My father told me many times that he was so happy to have sons.

Our family was so complete. We always had each other, and I never knew that the Hinton family wasn't a rich clan. My dad gave us a dime each day until we reached twelve years old. Then he gave us a quarter a day. My mother, full of wisdom, encouraged us to start a Christmas savings account at the local bank. I did that for about four years. Buying war stamps was also a way of saving, but when you are young, getting candy and going to the movies is always more exciting.

I took an interest in baseball at an early age. My sister Ruth and I used to take piano lessons every Thursday, but we had to practice during the time

MY TIME AT BAT — A STORY OF PERSEVERANCE

I was to play ball. Ruth continued to practice and went on to play for a church in Greensboro, North Carolina. However, I didn't reach the first grade in music because I just couldn't stand a game going on while I was practicing piano.

I stopped going to lessons, and I would use the money to go to the movies. After about two weeks of my doing this, my mom found out. Of course, this didn't sit well with her. She did what she always did when we did something wrong. She went to the switch. Mom would make us get our own switches. That was, unless we kept getting the very small ones.

Getting a whipping was not in itself so bad. The talking you got during and after it was the real punishment—words such as, "This hurt me more than you." The one that really got me was, "Shut up from crying." You would be hurting, but you had a limited time to cry. So you would suck it up and stop. If you didn't stop crying, you would get another whipping.

My mother was more than fair with all of us. She would let us get away with some things for a while, and then she would remind us of that while she whipped us. I couldn't understand how she could remember those things and in detail—even the day and date. If you got a spanking in school, or some other adult had to spank you or correct you, that was a doubleheader because you got it at home also.

Of course, I continued to play ball. When I was fifteen years old, I remember telling our director of recreation, D. J. Lenhardt, that I was playing for the local semi-pro team. He didn't approve of it because he thought they would misuse me and that I would start drinking or take up other bad habits. He also said, "You're not quite strong enough."

When he showed up at one of my games, on a Sunday after church, I just *had* to prove to him that I could take care of myself. I don't remember who won the game, but I do know that I did well enough to get his stamp of

My mother, Ada Hinton. 1951

How It All Began

approval. His words to me were, "You can play with them, but don't let them lead you into bad things." I thanked him for his approval. It meant more to me than almost anything I could think of. It gave me a sense of confidence in my ability, and I think it showed in my performance.

But being the oldest boy in our family took me away from baseball for a period. My mother's dad and his baby boy Herman, whom my brother Patches was named after, had a farm, and for part of the summer, we would go and help with the tobacco crop. Being the oldest boy, I had to spend one whole summer working there. It was by far the worst time of my life. There was no ball, just work. My mother had a time keeping my dad from coming and taking me home. Our family was just like my mother's: three boys and three girls. In my father's family, there were six boys and one girl. We didn't see a great deal of my dad's family because most of them moved from Rocky Mount at young ages.

My mother's dad lived in Nash County, only about fifteen miles away. I only worked there one summer because I told my dad that no baseball, no playing and no movies was not for a city boy, nor was it good for a future athlete. But I didn't need to tell him. After one time, thank God, he put his foot down and insisted I not go again. To this day, I think it was the only time I sided with my dad against my mom. I never heard my mom and dad say a cross word to each other; fighting and arguing were out of the question.

My mom worked one summer, maybe two, at the farm. She was busy at home teaching us about life. Some of the best advice my mother, a very religious woman, taught us was, "Take the chances life gives. Prove to yourself—and to the world—that you can do whatever you set your heart to, and always remember Jesus." My dad was such a provider. We always had what we needed. Beyond a shadow of a doubt, they both showed us love, support, pride and a God-fearing life. The apple doesn't fall far from the tree. I've given my family what my parents gave me. It's so easy to love people because they are people. This is a command from Jesus.

My father owned his own taxicab, which he would lend me on occasion. When I would keep it too long, Daddy would vow never to let me use it again. Momma would say, "Charlie, you needed the rest anyway." He'd always let me use it again, though.

MY TIME AT BAT — A STORY OF PERSEVERANCE

Daddy set his work schedule around our games. He attended almost every local game we played—and there were plenty...football, basketball and baseball for three sons. He was so supportive and proud of us all. He would brag excessively about what we had accomplished.

Momma loved to go to our basketball and baseball games. She would always attend the games that were against arch-rivals. She found them the most exciting. She liked to watch the crowd reacting to the game more than the game itself. However, she would never come to the football games. She said, "I don't know why you would want to play any game where the ambulance is waiting there for you." Everyone loved "Papason," as he was affectionately called, and our home was the local hangout. My father provided us with all kinds of modern conveniences—a TV, a refrigerator, a large stove and an indoor bathroom. Believe it or not, other families in our neighborhood did without these things.

Momma provided food. Boy, could she cook...and bake. Everyone would come to our house to eat because we always had plenty of food. After games, my mother would feed the entire team. For Thanksgiving and Christmas, she would bake each teammate his *own* favorite cake.

Growing up in Rocky Mount, we lived right behind a baseball field. Everybody played baseball. For as long as I can remember, I could catch, throw and hit a ball—any ball. That didn't change as I grew older. I always read up on baseball and did all I could to improve as a player.

As kids, we would go to the recreation center two blocks from our house to play sports. We called it the teenage center. During the winter, we would go to the gym and play basketball. There we learned to play Pinochle or Bid Whist while waiting for our team to play on the court. There were only two baskets; in fact, the local high school played its games and practiced there. Before the teenage center, the gym was the hangout, and D. J. Lenhardt was in charge at the time. His wife was the high school English teacher. At the teenage center, we played cards, ping-pong and pool every day.

Rocky Mount was split by a railroad that ran through the middle of downtown. On one side was Edgecomb County, and on the other side was Nash County. My section of Rocky Mount, called Crosstown, had everything: the gym, teenage center, high school, swimming pool, baseball park, two drug stores, two movie theaters, two pool rooms, two funeral homes,

How It All Began

two barber shops and a few other black-owned businesses. The town was so segregated that you didn't see white people until you went downtown. And with all the black-owned businesses, you only had to go downtown to get clothing. Most of the people had a connection to a relative's farm that was nearby, so food was plentiful. When you went to someone else's house, the first thing they asked you was, "Do you want something to eat?"

Even though some sections of Rocky Mount had a reputation for being bad, everybody, that is, black people, got along well, for we needed one another. Everyone spoke when they would meet or pass one another. Even blacks and whites did this; "hey" was the word. I had a time when I went to Washington and would speak to people and they didn't answer.

On Thanksgiving, we had an annual football game with Little Raleigh, a section of Rocky Mount. Most of the players on the high school team didn't play much because football season wasn't over yet. But since everyone in town knew about the traditional game, it was well-attended, and all had a good time. Everything went well. We played tackle football with no pads for about three hours. I don't remember anyone getting hurt bad enough to require a doctor.

ALL HAIL BOOKER T.

I had always been small, so football wasn't always my game. In fact, my first year at Booker T. Washington High School, I didn't even weigh a hundred pounds. People always thought Checo was older than I was, as he was quite stocky. Since I was so small, I joined the marching band, playing alto horn.

I started playing basketball my sophomore year and football my senior year–after I had gained about forty pounds. At first, I was a quarterback, but I threw so hard that no one could catch my balls. So I said, "I'll show you how to catch a ball" and switched to wide receiver. Ironically, I didn't get to play baseball in high school. The baseball program was discontinued after my freshman year.

Eventually, I was inducted into the Booker T. Hall of Fame, but not for baseball. Nevertheless, I got to play plenty of baseball. I started playing semipro ball when I was fourteen years old–a mere teenager among men. I

MY TIME AT BAT — A STORY OF PERSEVERANCE

Herman "Patches" Hinton shortly before his death. 1988

really had to hold my own. Checo also started playing when he turned fourteen. We played for all the local teams. When one team wasn't playing, we'd go across town to play for another.

Where was Patches? Following right behind us. In fact, as far back as I can remember, everywhere I went, Patches went—except when I was courting, of course. He learned a lot from watching us all those years, and he turned out to be quite an athlete himself.

WASHINGTON, D.C.—ALWAYS HOME

Washington, D.C. was like a second home to me. I used to travel to D.C. to work during the summer to buy school clothes. I would stay with my sister, Ellen Green, and her family. I had yet another opportunity to play baseball there. My brother-in-law, Herman Green, worked for the Veterans Administration. Herman's division at work had a baseball team I used to play on. I would take every opportunity I could to play baseball. Everywhere I turned, there was a team to join. I just believe the Lord had a plan for me. He made it possible for me to hone my skills so I would be ready when the opportunity presented itself. And it always did.

Proverbs 18:16 says, "A man's gift maketh room for him, and bringeth him before great men." I am a living testimony of that truth. I was gifted, and the Lord didn't allow those gifts to lie dormant inside of me. However, I did have to do my part. I just couldn't sit there with the gifts and expect scouts or coaches to come knocking on my door. I had to persevere.

After graduating from high school, I returned to Washington to work and to play more semipro baseball with the Maryland Wildcats, a young baseball team. Five of my teammates had previously played professional baseball, so I was able to learn a lot from them. As part of our game schedule, our team went on a southern trip, which included Rocky Mount. For

How It All Began

many years, everybody on the team talked about the way my parents fed them for two days.

During the game in Rocky Mount, there was a home run battle between Checo and me. I told the team he could hit a fastball as good as any player. Well, a pitcher, like a hitter, is confident and up to the challenge. He believes his fastball will not be hit. I am not one to say, "I told you so," but Checo hit two fastballs out of the park for home runs. I hit two inside-the-park home runs. We won the game easily 9-4, and everyone had a great time. All our players worked and played for their love of the game. In fact, I never received a dime, and we had some big crowds and a great following. We played every weekend. On trips, we drove our own cars and were glad to do so.

One of those moments that made it all worth it was during a game at Stafford, Virginia. Late in the game with the score tied, I hit a routine hit to right field. The right fielder booted the ball for an error. I took off for second base and slid. The throw was low and got by the shortstop. So I took off for third base and slid again. The throw there was off, and I got up again and headed for home plate. I slid again and was safe. It turned out to be the winning run. It was so funny.

MY BIG BEAR

Checo later went on to college at Shaw University. After his first semester, he urged me to attend Shaw. At first, I was reluctant because as the eldest son, I felt a responsibility to work. But Checo insisted: "I told the coach that you were an awesome catcher. Coach said he needs you. They'll give you a full baseball scholarship." So I packed my things and headed for Raleigh, North Carolina. At Shaw, Checo and I played baseball, football and basketball. I was small, but I was fast. In football, I played wide receiver and defensive end. In those days, you played defense *and* offense. You never got a break.

Checo was a terror–strong as an ox and tough as steel–and he talked much noise. He played offensive and defensive tackle. He was so good that after college, the New York Titans drafted him. However, during training camp, they traded him to the Boston Patriots. I later asked the coach, Sammy Barr, what happened. He said, "Man, we didn't want to trade him. He can block and hit with a vengeance, but we got two running backs for

My Time at Bat — A Story of Perseverance

him." Later, we would be inducted into Shaw University's Hall of Fame. The Hinton boys were a force to be reckoned with.

Before I arrived at Shaw, my brother had told everybody I was coming. I didn't have a problem adjusting because I started getting the baseball players together right away playing catch and scooping up short hops in the dorm hallway. I was a leader from the start, and I had every player putting in time that they would not have put in for anyone else, other than the coach.

Jim Lytle, our coach and athletic director, was a baseball lover at heart, so he loved what he saw and often heard about what we were doing. We worked hard on our game, and strange as it may sound, we were all on the same page. The coach never had a problem keeping the team late. He wanted to stay until dark every day we could be outside. When it rained, we were in the gym. The basketball players didn't like that, but when your coach is the director of athletics, you get the gym for as long as is necessary. We had 19 games, almost all of which were C1AA conference games. We were off to a great start. We were 9-0.

When we went on a northern swing, I was almost 155 pounds and starting catcher. But I was still small, compared to some players. During a collision at the plate, I lost to a Howard University player of about 210 pounds. His thigh hit my right shoulder, and I knew right away something was out of place. I was lost to the team for about two weeks, and the team lost every game. I played in the last two games at about forty percent arm strength. I could barely get the ball back to the pitcher, but I sure would fake it as if I had a missile.

Swinging didn't hurt my shoulder, so I had about three hits each game. But I was disappointed and felt as though I had let the team down. I could not even go with the team to away games. The team really missed me. At the college level, a team is lucky to have four, maybe six, good players–including the pitcher. Therefore, when you lose one of your star players, you lose a big part of the whole pie. It is unlike professional ball, where the manager can call any number of players from the bench who have the same skills. In college, when you lose a player, the skills are lost to the team, and there is no replacement for that season. In many cases, the entire season is shot.

How It All Began

Out of our starting nine players on the baseball team, all but one was also on the football team. Basketball was different. Only Checo, I and one other baseball player were on the team. I started some basketball games, but Checo was a force under the boards (grabbing rebounds), and boy could he shoot. Please don't get him started because to this day, he thinks he can still shoot.

I never had the size or strength he had. At age fourteen, he was hitting baseballs out of the park, while I would get inside-the-park home runs. But he had no concept of the strike zone and would swing at almost any pitch. He would rope a fastball a long way, although a curve ball would just about get him most of the time. This was so strange to me because I always felt nobody was going to throw a strike. I later found that was not true at the pro level.

I, unlike Checo, pride myself with knowing the strike zone, and seldom did I swing at a bad pitch. This worked for me. I was in my mid-teens before I had my first strikeout. Before that, I did not believe any pitcher, no matter who he was, could get three pitches by me. But it did happen during a recreational game. The pitcher was in his late teens and had an outstanding fastball. I think the count was two balls and two strikes when he threw a fastball that I took. The young umpire called me out. The pitch was outside, but my streak and strike-out record had ended. To make matters worse, I started to cry because I struck out.

I later learned that any pitcher in pro ball would blow you away anytime. It would have been very bad and even funny if I had done that in a big pro game. But my first strikeout taught me something–that you can't take a pitch even close to a strike when you already have two strikes.

Checo was also a strong force in football. I'll never forget one football game against Maryland Eastern Shore. One of Maryland's tackles clipped me from behind. Checo said, "That's all right. I'll get him." The next play, Checo blasted him with an elbow to his mouth. (Those days football helmets had just a single bar in front.) He fell to the ground. Blood was gushing from his mouth, and he was spitting out several teeth. I said, "Checo, did you try to kill the man, or what?" After the game, the player was asking around for Checo, "Where's that dirty tackle?" Checo said, "I don't know; he must have gotten on the bus."

My Time at Bat — A Story of Perseverance

Things were going pretty well at Shaw until we got the news that my father had passed away. That was a hard pill to swallow. My strong tower was gone. A year later, I missed him with a passion.

THE THINGS YOU DO FOR LOVE

When I was playing basketball at Shaw, I was excited when I learned we were scheduled to play Johnson C. Smith University one weekend. That's where Irma Elizabeth Macklin attended college. I knew her all my life. I called her Bunny. She was younger than I, and we didn't date until she was in high school. I continued to court her when she went to Charlotte to attend Smith. She was a debutante, elegant and beautiful–inside and out.

Irma Elizabeth Macklin my "Bunny" being crowned Debutante Queen.

Since the basketball team was headed her way, I hitchhiked to Charlotte ahead of time to see Bunny. I wanted to spend as much time with her as possible. She had a strict curfew–six o'clock–and the team usually left immediately after the game.

When I arrived at Bunny's dorm, it was after curfew. She had to talk to me from her dorm room window. At Smith those days, girls couldn't go anywhere without a chaperon. Fortunately, the next day was the dorm's movie day. All the ladies who were willing could go to the movies–with a chaperon, of course. We were so happy just to sit together at the theater. But after the movie, she had to go back to her dorm.

One of my teammates was from Charlotte, so I stayed at his

How It All Began

parents' house that night. The big game was the next day. I was excited that Bunny would get a chance to see me play. I was really going to show out. However, because I had hitchhiked to Charlotte without permission, the coach benched me. I'm sad to say, Bunny never got to see me play any of my college games.

When I got back to Shaw, I was reading *The Sporting New*s, a baseball weekly, and I saw that the New York Giants were holding a tryout in Frederick, Maryland. I said, "Checo, I'm going to the tryouts." When we got home, I told my mother I was going to take a chance.

Momma gave me one of the three dollars she had and sent me on my way with her blessing. That was all I needed to head out to the highway with my heart full of hope. I hitched a ride with a truck driver all the way to Washington, D.C, some 245 miles. When he ate, I ate. Once we got to D.C., I headed to my sister Ellen's apartment.

Chapter Three

Following My Dream

I started out early for Frederick for the tryouts. I was so excited I could hardly stand it. I had so much confidence—and was eager to show them what I could do. I had no doubt that I would be signed. I felt that I had a great chance at a tryout held by an individual team, primarily because there are far fewer prospective players trying out—around seventy-five.

It turned out to be relatively easy to get to D.C., but getting from D.C. to Frederick—a mere thirty miles—proved to be the biggest challenge. There I was on the highway, still beaming with expectation.

It took me three hours and at least five rides hitching to get to Frederick. When I finally arrived at the tryouts, they were finishing up for the day. I spoke with the head scout, who said I could come back the next day. I was terribly disappointed, but there was still hope for tomorrow.

When It Seems Like Hope Is Gone

I asked around to find out who was going back to D.C. A pitcher spoke up and gave me a ride back to Ellen's house. He assured me that he would

My Time at Bat — A Story of Perseverance

pick me up the next morning to return to the tryouts. I was to meet him on the corner at eight thirty. I was there before eight o'clock. He never showed up. I was devastated and heartbroken. The only other time I hurt that bad was when my father died. All my hopes were seemingly shattered.

Fortunately, I read in *The Daily News* that a major tryout was being held at Griffith Stadium the next week. However, this time all the Major League teams would be scouting. Therefore, instead of seventy-five players competing for their attention, there were 700. I wondered how all those players were going to be noticed. Well, I decided to give them a show, and that I did.

TRIAL BY FIRE

I was a catcher with great speed–unlike most stocky catchers. The first thing I did was dazzle them in the sixty-yard dash, which I ran in 6.5 seconds. Each player was given a number and then assigned to a group of four other players. There would be a complete infield–a catcher, first baseman, second baseman, third baseman and shortstop–in each group. We would field the ball and try to make an indelible impression in the short time we had.

To this day, I am proud of the way I lit up the stands. I heard "Oooo" and "Aahh" from the stands all day...and we were there all day...without a break...without lunch... I could catch with the best of them, and I really got a chance to show them my ability. I was so impressive that the scouts insisted I hit first–catchers usually hit eighth. "No," they said, "we want to see *him* hit!"

Well, I was in my element. Sometimes you are in the right place at the right time, doing what you do best. I was in "the zone," and I did everything well. At the end of the day, they called the numbers of all the players who were to return the next day for the exhibition game. Suddenly, 700 players whittled down to seventy-five, and I was one of the chosen few. They instructed us to return to the stadium at nine o'clock the next morning for "the show."

SHOW 'EM WHAT YOU GOT

You *know* I was there early! I arrived at eight o'clock for the exhibition game. I had my uniform on and was ready for a day's work. With all of the

Following My Dream

goings-on, I managed to stay calm and focused. Again, the scouts requested that I hit first in the game. That fit right in with my plan.

Deep down inside your heart, you have to believe in your own ability, no matter what. I had no problem hitting. If I could see the ball from the pitcher's hand to the plate, I believed I could hit it. In all my at-bats, no pitcher has ever thrown a ball I could not see—and I could always hit a curve ball.

My hand/eye coordination was sharp—way above average. I'm sure that *strike-out*—a game Checo and I played every day as youths—had something to do with that. One of us would throw bottle tops or small rocks, while the other hit until we missed. Checo would get mad and want to quit because I'd be hitting for fifteen to twenty-five minutes at a time. Occasionally, I'd let him hit first or I'd strike out intentionally to keep him playing with me. I often thank him for those times. Checo has been a big plus in my life.

RISING TO THE OCCASION

All day long at Griffith Stadium, I hit the ball hard. I had about seven at-bats and got on base each time, and I stole second and third. I played first base and outfield. A brother showed his skills that day. I spoke with countless scouts and told them I was in college but was willing to play in the Minor Leagues.

Many scouts pulled me to the side and said, "Don't you sign with anyone until you speak with me on Monday." Well, that didn't faze me a bit. A bird in the hand...is what my mother always taught me. Again, I had to think of my financial responsibilities. A scout from the Orioles, John "Pope" Whalen, gave me his card and told me to come to Baltimore at ten o'clock Monday morning. As usual, I hitchhiked to Baltimore for the meeting.

The Orioles signed me to play for their organization for $200 a month with a $500 bonus. Pope gave me $5 for lunch—that was my way back to D.C. My hitchhiking days were over. I was handed my very first airplane ticket to Arizona to play Class C ball for their Phoenix Suns in the Arizona-Mexican League.

Chapter Four

The Minor Leagues

My first airplane ride was exciting, but playing baseball was the only thing I could think about. When the plane landed, as instructed, I took a cab to the stadium. Then I was assigned to house with the other black players.

Since I was signed late, the season was half over when I arrived. When I got there, Wayne Coleman, from Asheville, North Carolina, and Rudy Thompson, from East St. Louis, welcomed me to the house. We each paid $10 a month to live there. They were happy when I arrived because I would share the expenses. Wayne, a shortstop, and Rudy, a first baseman, were both in their second year playing professional ball. Rudy had a car, so transportation was no problem. We definitely ate out a lot.

It was early afternoon, and we had to be at the stadium at around 5:30 P.M. for an 8 P.M. game. We played night games because of the hot weather. During the day, it would reach 110 to 120 degrees. It was not a problem for me. My first day, after meeting everyone and getting my uniform and locker belongings, I was full of enthusiasm and excitement.

My Time at Bat — A Story of Perseverance

RIDING THE BENCH

Yes, I was happy and proud to be there. But for the first time in my life, I had to sit, wait and watch what was going on. It was a really hard time for me, but I know that there is a time to keep your mouth closed, your ears open and learn whatever you can. It was a hard pill to swallow, but you do what you have to do. A whole week went by, and I had not played in a game. In fact, I was in the bull pen warming up the pitchers to go into the game.

I learned that being part of a team means you do the best you can. Always staying in shape is part of that team commitment—as is being alert during the game and knowing the count on the hitter and how many outs the team had. Since I was a catcher, I knew I would have to know what to do when I did get to play. While I was warming the bench, I learned our team's signs, including the signs I would have to give to the pitchers. I soon learned that asking too many questions was not cool. Therefore, I would wait until we black players got together to ask or talk about certain things.

We went off on our first road trip. The trip was about twelve days and, as always when on the road, we were given $2 a day for meals. You did have to budget your money, but in 1956, $2 was plenty if you knew where to go. I relied on Wayne and Rudy's knowledge of places to eat.

Whether we were on the road or at home, we got paychecks the first and fifteenth of every month. I was doing fine with $200 a month, since in 1956, the average salary was about half that–$25 per week. In addition, on the road, hotel expenses were covered. I was able to send money to my mother, now a widow, and my brothers, who were both in college at Shaw University in Raleigh, North Carolina, to buy school clothes and whatnot.

ROLL WITH THE PUNCHES

By this time, I had adjusted to the fact that I was a back-up catcher and my playing time was going to be limited. But the time came for me to play. We were at our first stop on the trip, Yuma, Arizona, and we were losing by seven runs in the fifth inning. The manager, Billy Capp, told me, "Grab a bat and pinch hit for the pitcher. Then put on your catcher's gear and catch."

The Minor Leagues

This is what I had been waiting for since the day I arrived. I was not as ready as I thought. I kept telling myself that I finally had the chance to prove myself. All my experiences flashed in my mind. However, to be focused, I had to put everything aside and deal with the moment.

I was announced as a pinch hitter. I was so eager to hit that I swung at the first pitch. It really looked good to me. I hit a fly ball to center field for an out. I was a little upset because I did not get a hit, but I knew I would get to bat again, as it was just the top of the sixth inning. I came back to the dugout and put on my catcher's gear.

MY FIRST PRO HIT

We began to rally and scored six runs. It was my turn to bat again with the tying run on second base. I do not recall if it was the first pitch or not, but I got a single and drove in the tying run. I thought I was flying, not running, because my feet felt so light. I was one happy camper! I had been on the team for more than a week, and only then did I feel as though I was really a part of it. The next batter got out.

When I came in to put on my catcher's gear, Capp told me the regular catcher was going to finish the game. I was not upset because I had learned to roll with the manager's decisions. At any level of play, the manager makes the moves he deems necessary to win the game. I was just so happy to have gotten my first hit and RBI and to have tied the game. Therefore, I was undaunted. We went on to win that game, and I was a large part of it.

I was now a real pro with proof that I belonged. Oh, what a thrill it was. The next day, I could hardly wait to see the newspapers. I could not wait to see my name and read what was written up about my first hit and tying RBI. I sent about five articles home.

I MISS YOU, POP

When we left Yuma, we went to Douglas, Arizona. In the second game, our catcher stumbled on first base and skinned himself up pretty bad. That meant I was now the catcher. I can't begin to tell you how elated I was or how I'd longed for that moment. I could just hear my father saying, "All the hype is over; you're the man now. You got to run this game, call the pitches

MY TIME AT BAT — A STORY OF PERSEVERANCE

My father, Charlie Hinton, Sr. 1955

you want the pitcher to throw, and take charge."

It is heartbreaking that my father passed away only one year before I made it to the pros. He never got a chance to see me realize *our* dream. He was constantly on my mind. I felt I couldn't let him down. I am sure that my father was a large factor in my success–he really believed in me, encouraged me and gave me a sense of pride. Had he been alive when I was playing pro ball, no one would have been able to stand him–he would have gloated all day about his boy.

In all my years, I was never more proud to put on catcher's gear and go into a game. I took on the responsibility of catcher in stride. As far as I was concerned, no one could do it better than I. I wasn't being overconfident; I had been catching for more than ten years. I knew I could handle the pitcher with ease. A good catcher must have the confidence of the pitcher. He must not only call the pitches, but he must know his pitcher straight up and call the right pitch to set up the out pitch.

It is a fact that I had done my homework and I was a good handler of pitches. I also had a good throwing arm and was quick on my feet. I had great hands, and I took pride in blocking low balls in the dirt. I was proud that I could do the job. I watched, learned and studied to develop my craft. I was a leader, and I showed that I knew what I was doing. Most of all, I loved what the job called for and was able to deliver. On top of it all, the next day, I went two for four and had an RBI.

MY FIRST START

From Douglas, the team headed off to Mexicali, Mexico, where I was still the starting catcher. The second day of the trip, I went three for four and

The Minor Leagues

hit my first and only home run of the season. We won that game, and the feeling I had is indescribable. I was having a ball, playing every day. I performed better than most thought I would.

After we got back to Phoenix, our regular catcher was ready to come back, and the manager asked me if I would play the outfield. My answer was, "No question!" I didn't have a problem with that. I determined that I would play outfield with excellence as well. I played right field, and before I knew it, the season was ending.

My Minor League experience was a very happy one. I learned many things about baseball, but also about life and people. We had a good team, and we finished the season in second place in the league and only a little behind Tucson, Arizona. I knew I had opened some eyes and as a rookie, I had skills. I learned what a team really is and how to be ready at all times, whether in the game or not.

After the season's end, I could hardly wait to get home and tell everyone that I had a great two months in the Minor Leagues—and got my $500 bonus. My record was G-29, AB-85, H-23, R-12, 2B-4, 3B-1, HR-1, RBI-11, with a .271 batting average.

THE LOVE OF MY LIFE

I was signed, fulfilling a life-long ambition to play professional baseball. After my first season, I wanted to tell anyone who would listen that I had just had the time of my life, and baseball was the reason. After arriving home, my first order of business was to go see Bunny, my sweetheart. I was now earning a living and able to support a family. I was anxious to get started, so I asked Bunny to marry me.

There was one problem, though: She was in college, and we knew her family would not want her to quit. We decided that our need for each other was greater, so we eloped to Greensboro, North Carolina. I wrote her mother a nice letter to let her know that this was no fly-by-night rendezvous. I loved Bunny and intended to spend the rest of my life with her.

My sister Ruth and her family were living in Greensboro. We told my sister and her husband, Jesse, that we were getting married, and they made room for us. We were married on October 1, 1956. Marrying Miss Irma E.

Macklin was the best decision I ever made. Our love has grown over the years. It is even better now than in 1956. Throughout our marriage, God and Jesus have been our guide. Within two weeks' time, I took a job at the mill where Jesse worked and was pleased as punch to have a wife and a new baseball career.

YOU'RE IN THE ARMY NOW

Things couldn't have been better. But wouldn't you know it? I received a letter from ol' Uncle Sam a month later. He was requesting my services in the Armed Forces. I definitely did not want to go, even though we were in between the Korean and Vietnam wars.

When I arrived in Fort Benning, Georgia, I let the first sergeant know that I had played in the Minors and wanted to go out for the Army team. To my surprise, he told me I could not be on the team, for some inexplicable reason. I went to the gym and spoke with the coach, and he was livid. I said, "Hey, don't get me into trouble. I was just having a conversation with you."

The next thing I knew, I heard, "Private Hinton, please report to the field" blaring over the public address system. I was assigned to the Special Forces, and we had a ball. All I had to do was play baseball and practice. We weren't assigned to any other work detail. When I got stationed in Fort Bragg, North Carolina, I was so glad to be close to home, just seventy-six miles from Rocky Mount. Bunny and I had just gotten a Chevrolet we called Bessie, and we went to Rocky Mount every chance we got. They were so lenient in the Special Forces that one time we got carried away and stayed in Rocky Mount for three days.

ARE YOU AWOL, OR WHAT?

When we returned to Fort Bragg, my buddy was sitting on my front porch. "Where have you been?" he asked. "They've been looking all over for you!" I put on my fatigues, which I never had to wear, and reported in. I was wondering, Where am I going to tell this man I've been? I am definitely going to be court-marshaled and sent to the brig.

The Minor Leagues

Before I got a chance to speak, the officer said, "Where have you been? We want you to play softball!" I sighed...deeply. I had never really played softball, but I went out and played so well that the coach asked me, "What do you want?" I said, "I want to go home to Rocky Mount." "Done," he said, as he wrote me a pass for an entire week.

When baseball season was over, I didn't want to leave the Special Forces. I didn't look forward to digging ditches or whatever hard labor tasks the other companies were assigned to do. So I joined the football team. In my first game, I intercepted a ball and ran it in for a touchdown.

THE ORIOLES TAKE ANOTHER LOOK

In the meantime, I wrote to the Orioles to let them know I was doing my patriotic duty. They arranged for me to come up to Baltimore for batting practice. When I got there, the manager was unfamiliar with my play since I had played in Phoenix. I was hitting everything in site. Again, they were impressed and assured me that my place on the team was secure.

I finished out my two years with the Army. That experience was memorable. We had a bunch of fun and met some wonderful people. A few future Major Leaguers were on the Army baseball team with me–including John Wyatt and Grover Deacon Jones. As it turned out, 1956 was an eventful year in my life. I went from college to professional baseball, married my sweetheart and was drafted into the Army.

Chapter Five

The High Life

When I left the Army, I headed to Thomasville, Georgia, for the Orioles' Minor League camp. I was surprised to find out that of the twenty-five players there with me two years ago, all but four had been released. These were very good players. I knew I had to get it going early and keep it going. Seeing players released and sent home was not a pleasant thing to experience. Even after just one week, players were being released. It was sad, but that's the nature of the business. Some cuts you agree with; others you do not. And you do miss certain players who have been released, but you have to put that aside and take care of yourself. If you were good enough to make it through spring training, you were assigned to a team, then transported to that city to start league play.

At the pro level, race didn't play as large a role as one might think. For the most part, a player was judged on his talent. Many times, the decision about who would stay and who would go was difficult, and the outcome was not always popular. If they had equal or almost equal talent, white players were chosen over black players. If you were black and playing in the pros, it goes without saying that you were definitely very good.

My Time at Bat — A Story of Perseverance

At the Minor League camp, I was told that I hit too well and ran too fast to be a catcher. So I was assigned to third base and then to the outfield. I have to admit that I was disappointed, for catching was my first love. The catcher is the only player who faces every player on the opposing team. He is the leader. Not only does he have to know his pitching staff, he has to study each batter and work with the pitcher's strengths to keep the batter off stride. The catcher has to switch up his methods and stance. He can't do the same thing every play. The catcher and pitcher must remain unpredictable. Furthermore, I was fast…very fast…and the manager thought I shouldn't damage my knees by catching. Many a catcher will tell you that their knees will never let them forget that they had been a catcher.

As a catcher, I was strongly influenced by the great Josh Gibson. He was a great home run hitter who played for the Homestead Graves of the Negro League. He was an outstanding catcher who could throw base runners out while still squatting. When he died in 1948, Roy Campenella became my inspiration as a catcher. "Campy," a Hall of Famer, really made me want to be a catcher.

MAKING ADJUSTMENTS

I came to realize that the club was right to change my position in the field. I got over my disappointment and went on to prove that I could make the adjustment without missing a beat. I took plenty of fly balls and began to be very comfortable in the outfield. But I did have to make an adjustment and work at mastering the position. In practice, balls were batted from the player's hand to the outfield. However, during a game, an outfielder has to get into fielding position and focus on the ball coming off the bat.

You learn from practice and experience where the ball is going and whether it will be catchable; that's called getting a jump on the ball. You have to know the wind, the sun, the lights and the stadium to gauge the flight of the ball. If the ball gets by the infield, the outfielder has to make the play to keep the batter from advancing to the next base. You have to support the pick-off plays by always anticipating a bad throw and being in the right spot at the right time, ready to back up the throw before it happens.

I knew I wouldn't last long if I weren't willing to learn my trade and work on being the best I could be. You have to show what you can do when

The High Life

the play is yours. You must haul your share of the load and make the plays when the game is on the line. I had to prove myself, repeatedly, on a daily basis.

I loved meeting the other players. You share a camaraderie and common goal perfecting your craft and moving on to the next level.

1959–A BANNER YEAR

After surviving all the cuts, thirty of us were sent to Aberdeen, South Dakota, to play for manager Earl Weaver. That season was pure joy. My wife was finally with me—they discouraged wives from coming to spring training so young players could stay focused. And I even got to catch a few games.

I had never seen so many white people. In fact, Joe Pullium and I were the only black players on the team. We would walk down the street, and cars would stop and stare at us as though looking for a tail or the color to fall off. Kids used to sit on top of the dugout. When I would go to bat or come in, they would rub my hair or touch my skin. After they touched me, they would look at their hands to see whether the color came off, as they had not seen or been around black people. It was funny to me.

In any event, that didn't distract me from the game. I do not think I was ever below a .330 batting average all year. I had a hard time, but I did catch and, at the end, pass the league's leading hitter. In fact, I think it was next to the last day when I did. I ended up with a .358 average and a win by two points. The team finished second in the league. I also had twenty-two home runs and 108 RBIs. It was hard not to have fun.

Besides league batting champion, in 1959, I was the Rookie of the Year and the league's Most Valuable Player. On top of all that, I was too excited that Bunny was expecting our first child.

I was told that the Orioles listed me highly in their organization and intended to send me to the winter Instructional League in Clearwater, Florida. That league was for a team's prize Minor League players, to bring out their potential. Major Leaguers could go too if they had injuries and were on the disabled list a certain length of time. The league was first set up for the top prospects, mainly bonus players. I was selected to go because I

MY TIME AT BAT — A STORY OF PERSEVERANCE

ORIOLE EYE-POPPERS—Three members of the Baltimore Winter League team that have been keeping the flock near the top and providing rosy dreams for visiting Baltimore brass are: (from left) first baseman, John (Boog) Powell; left fielder, Pete Ward, and second baseman, Charlie Hinton.

was an all-around player who could hit, throw, field and run very well. It was a big deal to go to the Instructional League because everyone wanted to get as much training as possible. The ultimate dream was to go to "The Show"–the Major Leagues–and this was only the dress rehearsal. Charlie Beamon was in Clearwater with me that winter of 1959. He was a pitcher but was there to play as an outfielder.

When I left for Clearwater, Bunny went to New York to stay with her mother, Tas Hannah. For the first time, it was hard to focus on baseball. I was concerned with her safety and the health of our unborn child. I managed to have a good fall session, though. I played five positions, including catcher, batted .300 and stole a bunch of bases. Overall, I had a great time and proved to be a complete baseball player.

JUST CALL ME 'BIG DADDY'

I didn't get to see my son until one month after he was born. He was a big, well-built baby, with a pleasant disposition and huge hands. His hands and feet looked just like mine, but his face resembled that of my brother Patches. As a toddler, my son looked just like my father. He was my namesake, Charles Edward Hinton III, "Chucky," my proudest accomplishment to date.

Chucky always has been one of the nicest people you could ever meet. His sisters often say they couldn't have asked for a better big brother. He is

The High Life

a man without guile. You'd never hear him speaking ill of someone or being petty. He's what you call a *good* person, and he's wise. Having children was the most beautiful experience of my life.

Meanwhile, I headed to Miami, Florida, for spring training with Baltimore's AAA team. I mainly played second base and was among the top players. I was assigned to Vancouver, Baltimore's AAA team in the Pacific Coast League. By now, I was being paid $500 a month and was a proud father and husband.

A month into the season, I was called into the manager's office and told that I was being sent to Stockton, California, to play C-Class baseball. To my surprise, the manager said, "As soon as you start

Chucky and I playing in the Senators' Father and Son Game. Chucky, the youngest kid playing at three years old, became the star of the game when he slid at each and every base. The crowd cheered wildly. 1962

hitting like you should, we'll bring you back." My mouth dropped open. Was this a demotion? I couldn't conceive of it.

In Stockton, I had to prove myself again. I was moved to the outfield. Hank Bevins and I were the only black players. I was in Stockton for the rest of the season, and I did not understand why. I was determined not to worry about things out of my control. What I could control was my level of play.

I think I was there for 101 games. I hit .600 the first month, .500 the next month and .400 the following month. At one time, I stole thirty-seven bases without being thrown out, and I ended up with eighty-eight RBIs. Again in 1960, I was league batting champion with a .369 average. I now held back-to-back batting titles. I was an All-Star and again the league's Most Valuable Player. As a team, we finished right at the top of the league.

Yet, I was a lonely man.

MY TIME AT BAT — A STORY OF PERSEVERANCE

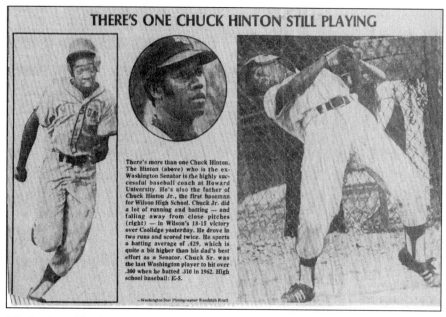

My first born Chucky was quite a baseball player in high school. 1977

Bunny was expecting our second child, and I wanted her mother to watch over her. We decided it was best, so Bunny and Chucky went to New York to be with Tas. Our phone bill was astronomical because we talked every day. She was not only my wife, the mother of our children, but to this day, she is my everything.

But I do not have to tell you how much fun I had playing the game. I was player of the week and player of the month on more than one occasion. Playing baseball was never work to me.

And I learned the team and winning came first. I have seen many players come and go. It was not easy at times. But the bottom line is you have to take care of yourself. There are certain things you do not like, but you have to deal with the bad and the good.

CHANCE OF A LIFETIME

Next I headed over to Scottsdale, Arizona, and had another good season with the top players. To my knowledge, I still own the Orioles record for Overall Hitting in a Minor League Career with an average of .333. About

The High Life

halfway through the season, I had been put on the Orioles Major League roster of forty. I was elated.

In effect, I finally had graduated to the Major Leagues. I was now draftable. But the Orioles did not think anyone would draft me because I hadn't played long in the Minor Leagues. In a ploy to keep me with their organization and to discourage other teams from drafting me, the Orioles circulated rumors that I had a broken shoulder. The Orioles' scheme did not work; they were surprised when the Washington Senators drafted me for $75,000 in late 1960. I was one of 28 players the Senators drafted from the eight existing American League teams. I had made it to the big leagues.

OUR LITTLE FLOWER

The day I got home from the Instructional League, Bunny went into labor, and we had our first daughter, Jonquil Elizabeth. She looked just like me...for one week. Then she was the spitting image of my mother. As a toddler, she began to favor Bunny's mother—she certainly was a grandmammas' girl. Chucky couldn't pronounce Jonquil; all he could manage was Joni. Hence, "Joni" became her nickname. She was so precious and lovable.

Joni was Bunny's little helper when my last two daughters were born. She would change diapers and warm the babies' milk just as good as Bunny or I. Bunny called her "little mama." She was always bright and energetic.

Jonquil married George Branch. From that union was born my grandsons George "Tre" Branch and Eric Christopher Branch. In 1988, Joni married John Hawkins.

FOUR PORTS PLAYERS ON ALL-STARS

Chuck Hinton, Stockton's do-everything centerfielder, has been named to the California League All-Star team along with three other members of the first place Ports.

The team was announced today by league president Eddie Mulligan.

Also named to the 18-man squad were catcher Frank Zupo, shortstop Fred Scott, and pitcher Hal Woods.

Hinton, along with Bakersfield's Gary Kroll and Rich Edwards, Fresno's Dan Rivas, and Modesto's Elvio Jiminez were unanimous choices.

PLAY RENO

The All-Stars will oppose first half champion Reno in a game next Tuesday at Reno. The game was originally scheduled for July 16 but was moved up to avoid scheduling conflicts.

The star-studded squad will be managed by Buddy Kerr, Fresno, and Lou Kahn, Bakersfield, who recived an equal number of votes from the sportswriters and broadcasters.

18 SWIPES

Hinton has virtually been a one-man wrecking crew since joining the Ports from Vancouver. The speedy 24-year old Rocky Mount, N.C. flychaser has swiped 18 consecutive bases in 36 games through Wednesday without having been thrown out. He was batting a .360 clip with 28 RBI's, six homers, seven doubles, and four triples.

35

MY TIME AT BAT — A STORY OF PERSEVERANCE

My second child, Jonquil Elizabeth Hawkins and grandson Eric. Howard University Hospital asked Joni to bring Eric in for this picture. They posted it in a mural of their "Miracle Babies". 1986

Eric is a soldier. He was born weighing one pound, fifteen ounces, with Cerebral Palsy. The doctors didn't give him much chance to live. However, he held on.

Eric had to stay in an incubator for five months before he could come home. He struggled through two collapsed lungs, two strokes and double pneumonia. He wasn't expected to walk, talk, go to school or live a normal life. It was so hard for Joni to see Eric this way because her first son, George, died of Sudden Infant Death Syndrome. But she persevered and taught Eric to do the same.

Eric proved all the doctors wrong. He is a most vivacious and outgoing young man. Because of the strokes he suffered, he lost some functioning on his right side, but you can't tell him he has a disability. He plays basketball, football and volleyball with as much competitiveness as me. To top it off, he does well in school and is always one of the most popular kids. Everybody knows Eric.

I have to tell you about the Special Olympics 100 Meter Race Eric participated in. He was the only child in the race with a physical disability. Eric fell flat on his face at the start and skinned his knees, elbows—and pride. Before anyone could tell him anything, he got up and started running with all his might. He passed up most of the runners and finished third. Had the race been just a few yards longer, Eric would have won that race. He held up his bronze medal and said, "This is just like the gold to me!" Later, he did win a gold medal in the long jump. That boy has heart.

Chapter Six

The Expansion Washington Senators

My new team was part of the first expansion to take place in Major League Baseball. At first, the idea of expansion was met with reluctance.

In 1901, there were sixteen Major League Baseball teams: eight each in the National League and the newly created American League. Prior to 1958, there was big-league baseball in the Midwest (Chicago, Cleveland, Cincinnati, Detroit, Milwaukee, Kansas City and St. Louis), but only Minor League teams on the West Coast. That all changed in 1958, when the Brooklyn Dodgers moved to Los Angeles and the New York Giants moved to San Francisco, opening new markets in California. Jet travel was making the West Coast more accessible, and television was bringing far-away places into the living rooms of more Americans. At this point, more cities wanted Major League Baseball franchises, but Baseball was unwilling to increase the number of teams.

In 1959, Branch Rickey proposed the formation of a Continental League. The new league would have teams in New York, Minneapolis-St. Paul, Atlanta, Houston, Dallas, Denver, Buffalo and Toronto, and would compete with the current Major League teams for players, television revenue and fan support. Members of Congress, hoping to bring baseball teams to their home districts, hinted that Major League Baseball's antitrust exemption might be in jeopardy if the team owners continued to resist expansion. It was time for a change.

The Major League owners met in New York on October 26, 1960, to finalize plans for the first expansion in the history of the Major Leagues. It was decided that the American League would expand to ten teams in 1961, with the National League following suit in 1962. The two new American League cities would be Minneapolis and Los Angeles. The traditional 154-game schedule would be extended to 162 games, with teams playing each other 18 times a year instead of the 60-year standing of 22.

Washington Senators owner Calvin Griffith had been unhappy with his situation in Washington. Since the death of his adoptive father, Clark, in 1955, Griffith had been seeking to move his Senators out of the nation's capital. The other owners wanted to keep a team in Washington, so they denied his request to relocate. But with the addition of the two new teams, Griffith was given the okay to move his team to Minneapolis. The vacancy in Washington was filled by one of the new expansion entries. On November 17, 1960, the new Washington franchise was awarded to a hastily gathered group of ten local investors headed by General Elwood R. "Pete" Quesada, an administrator with the Federal Aviation Administration.

The Senators Inc. immediately went to work, hiring Ed Doherty as general manager and former Senators first baseman Mickey Vernon as field manager. On November 28, they acquired their first players (pitchers John Gabler and Ray Semproch) via the first Minor League draft. The next day, the new management signed free-agent infielder Dannie O'Connell and Coach Rollie Hemsley to contracts. Tom McKenna signed on as the team's trainer. The fledgling Senators were on their way and spent the next two weeks evaluating players who were made available for the first Major League expansion draft to fill the rosters of the two new teams.

> *"People gave you who they didn't want. I'm not going to say that I was in that category, but as far as the Orioles were concerned, I guess I was. They never thought I would be drafted, so that's one reason they put me on the list. Dean Chance was put up there, too, and we know what he became."*–Chuck Hinton

The Expansion Washington Senators

On December 14, 1960, the draft was held in Boston. The Senators selected a mixture of experience and youth, choosing players ranging in age from 22 (Bud Zipfel) to 38 (Gene Woodling). I was among those players. The league owners looked to the new season with apprehension. How would these new teams do with players that the existing teams were willing to lose? Would they be competitive, or would they play so poorly that the entire expansion experiment would be an artistic as well as a financial disaster? It was too late to turn back. The new Senators opened their first spring training camp on February 22, 1961, in Pompano Beach, Florida.[1]

---

[1] This chapter was excerpted from *Washington's Expansion Senators (1961–1971)*, by James R. Hartley, Corduroy Press, Germantown, MD. Used by permission.

MY TIME AT BAT — A STORY OF PERSEVERANCE

I first became aware of Chuck Hinton when I was 10 years old. It was 1961, and the "new" Washington Senators, an expansion team to replace the team that had just moved to Minnesota, were at spring training. I remember pictures of a slender outfielder wearing named Chuck Hinton wearing a very baggy uniform #51. The Senators had inherited the uniforms of the old club, and #51 had been worn by manager Cookie Lavagetto the previous year.

The story behind Chuck's selection in the expansion draft had been particularly interesting. He'd had a monster year in 1960 at Stockton in the California League, batting .369, and the Orioles, who owned his contract, wanted to keep him, but didn't want to have to protect him in the expansion draft. So they concocted a story that Chuck had been injured, so as to lessen interest in him. The new Senators drafted him anyway, and while he didn't go north with the big club in April, he got the call in May after a hot start at Indianapolis. Major league pitching proved no obstacle to Chuck, as he hit a very respectable .260 his rookie year, and did a good job in the outfield wearing #32.

Chuck's sophomore season, 1962, was quite simply, the best all-around offensive season an expansion Senator ever had. He batted .310 with 25 doubles, 17 home runs and 75 runs batted in, scoring 73 times and stealing 28 bases. He was clearly the best player on the club. He continued to shine the next 2 seasons–he made the all-star team in 1964–but was traded to Cleveland at the winter meetings in December 1964 for Bob Chance and Woodie Held. Chance was an overweight first baseman who struck out a lot, and Held was a veteran whose best years were behind him. Bad deal for the Senators, not to mention the fact that Chuck had started his insurance agency by that time, and I recall thinking that his customers would now have to call him long distance to file a claim, which is how a 13 year old looks at things.

The Expansion Washington Senators

I have a few specific memories of Chuck as a player. He broke up Joel Horlen's no-hitter in the 9th inning on July 29, 1963, and Don Lock homered thereafter, giving the Senators a 2-1 win. I remember Chuck's willingness to play anywhere, and with the Senators he played every infield and outfield position. Later, with the Indians, he got a chance to catch as well. I rooted for Chuck even when he wasn't wearing a Senators' uniform, though he did break my heart in a game in 1970 at RFK Stadium. The Senators were ahead 2-1 in the top of the 9th and the Indians were at bat. They got a man on base when Darold Knowles, the Senators bullpen ace, was called on the close it out. Tribe manager Al Dark sent Chuck up to pinch hit. He promptly homered over the centerfield fence and Cleveland won the game. I would surely have been more upset about it had it been anyone but Chuck.

I got to know Chuck when I began my on-air broadcast career in Washington in the late 1970's. I aked if he'd be a guest on my show, and he readily agreed. He was so real, so genuine on the air—so many athletes try to be something they're not when they're being interviewed—that we hit it off and have been, I'm happy to say, good friends since. I've done radio shows with Chuck many times since, but have also enjoyed his company and conversation well beyond the range of a microphone.

Chuck Hinton is, to date, the best African-American ballplayer in Washington Senators history. He and Frank Howard are the two most remembered position players from the expansion years. Beyond the American League, Chuck made an impact as a college coach at Howard. (One of his former players is my dentist!) I'm proud to call him my friend, and can only hope that he's going to be around for many, many years to come.

–Phil Wood
April 2002

Chapter Seven

On Stage at the Show

My first Major League spring training was in Pompano Beach, Florida, in February 1961. There were three other black players besides me on the team. Since blacks were not allowed to stay at the hotel with the white players, the Senators rented a house for us in the black section of town. This was thirteen years after Jackie Robinson broke the color line to become the first black Major League player. However, segregation continued in baseball until 1964.

At my first Major League spring training, with the Washington Senators, I was happy and full of pride. A rookie's expectations of himself, his team and the upcoming season are high. After all, those players at Major League spring training are among the best players baseball has to offer. Every day, I did what the team told me to do and completed my work in a business-like fashion.

Spring training was only thirty-five miles from Miami, where the Sir John Hotel was the blacks' meeting place. We could go there two or three times a week to be with players from other teams. I was not a drinker, so I would sip a beer most of the night, talking baseball with some of the greatest players in the sport.

I remember sitting with Elston Howard, Hank Aaron, Frank Robinson, Vada Pinson and so many others. It was like the Who's Who in Baseball. I would listen with all ears and take in all the info I could. Most of the stars were willing to let me in on any tips.

Hank would always have his hand-squeezer with him. He had some of the biggest hands I had ever seen. You have to remember that baseball players were discouraged from weight-lifting. Everyone, including players, coaches and trainers, said it would make a player muscle-bound—meaning not flexible or too tight to even swing a bat. Of course, that has been found to be far from the truth. Today, everyone lifts weights. Had I followed Hank's lead and strengthened my hands and wrists, maybe I would have hit many more home runs.

I was not one who made people uncomfortable by talking too much, although I had as much pride and belief in my skills as the next player. I knew that the Major League life was for those who could perform in almost any situation. I also knew that I had to show and do the right things at the right times no matter how the cards seemed to be stacked against me. Anyway, I felt nothing but love from the other black players, no matter how much they had accomplished.

I loved being part of the guys who gathered and talked over the games at the Sir John Hotel. There were only a few teams that didn't train in Florida, so I got to rub elbows with so many black players. We were a happy bunch and did what we could to help one another. We would even tell one another where we could buy clothes, shoes and sweaters. In other words, we shared information that would help us be proud Major League players. Black players took great pride in the way they dressed. We not only could play, but it was important to dress well and look good.

1961–EVERYTHING A FIRST

Of course, everything in 1961 was new and exciting to me because it was my first—my first everything. I would be talking and playing with the stars I read about. Things just could not have been better. I have to admit that it all

On Stage at the Show

caught me by surprise. Looking over everything and everybody, I knew it was only a matter of time before I would be in the "bigs."

The first three days of spring training consisted of intra-squad team play. I led off with a home run. My next at-bat was a bunted base hit. During exhibition play against other teams, I had a good average and was the talk of the camp. However, when a week and a half went by and I was not put in the lineup, I became a little concerned. Then when we went to Tampa to play the Cincinnati Reds, I started.

That day, I hit two home runs and two doubles. Didn't I blow their minds! Camp was about to end, and I had just hit four for four. I just knew I would be on the team. I was called in to the office for what I thought was the good news. Instead, I was told that of the outfielders, I was the only one without Major League experience. The Senators were on their way North to start the season, and I was not going with them. I simply said, "I understand. I'll be there soon...to stay."

Since the newly formed Senators had no Minor League farm team, I was on loan to the Cincinnati Reds, where I played center field, to gain more experience. I waited for the Senators to call for what seemed like an eternity. All the while, I was thinking, How could they keep me up here this long? I want to go to *The Show*! I worked hard and dedicated myself to sharpening my skills. I wanted to give the fans their money's worth by performing as a skilled Major Leaguer.

The time I spent in the Minor League AAA division went by quickly. I was hitting .320 and having the time of my life. Five weeks later, when the Senators called me back to the Major Leagues, I was ready to go. The Senators had a doubleheader scheduled against the Boston Red Sox. I was assigned to left field and up to bat third. Only the best batter hits third. How strange was that? First, I don't get signed because I have no experience, then five weeks later, I'm hitting third and am recognized as a great hitter. I was in the Major League to stay.

I arrived at my sister Ellen's apartment at about four-thirty in the morning. I went to bed to get a few hours of sleep before the games, but I could not fall asleep. It just wouldn't happen.

The next morning someone called out, "It's time for breakfast." I was already clean and ready to go. When I arrived at the clubhouse, it was so good to see all those guys. Everyone shook my hand and welcomed me to the team. In fact, from the time I went to the field until the game was over, there were so many people supporting me and wishing me well. I just played it real cool. After all, this was what I had always wanted. I had worked hard, listened and learned the game. *Oh, Baby!* This was the show! Here I was! This was just the beginning.

We started batting practice before the games. When that was over, I stayed to watch the Red Sox hit. Then we began to warm up for infield practice. After that, we went in to change our uniforms before the first game. You had to change before a game even if a little spot was on your uniform. You did this and whatever else you had to do in preparation for the game. When possible, you would watch the opposing team's pitcher warm up. You would try to pick up the pitcher's release point and see how much his breaking ball was breaking. Studying the pitcher before a game was helpful because you could pick up something to give you an edge.

The starting lineup was announced, and it was almost game time. The national anthem was played, and the pitcher finished his last warm-up. The first pitch was thrown, and the game was under way. For eleven years, from my first day in pro ball to my last, I always prayed during the national anthem. When the game got under way, I was fine. We got the Red Sox out in order, and I came running in to get ready to hit.

SHAKE IT UP, BABY

I got my bat, stood at the front steps of the dugout, and began eyeing the pitcher. After the first batter made an out, I went to the on-deck circle to get the leaded bat and some pine tar to loosen up. I kept my eyes on the pitcher. When the second batter got out, I headed toward the batter box. Then it happened. When announced to hit, I began to shake and quake. I didn't know what was happening. All I could do was pretend to have things under control.

That was all an act. This had never happened to me during anything I'd faced in my life. I was talking to my body…to no avail. I tried to stall by stepping out of the batter's box to get a sign from the third base coach. That did not do any good. In fact, I seemed to shake even more. I just tried to

On Stage at the Show

focus on the pitcher's release point. I was so shaken up that I did swing, but I hit a lazy fly ball for an out.

Well, I was a bit relieved that the first at-bat was over, and I could get myself together in the outfield. Someone brought me my glove, and I headed to left field, fussing with my body for doing this to me. I knew I didn't have a chance if I continued in this fashion–with my knees knocking, my body shaking.

I couldn't believe that I made another out my second at-bat. I was so mad because I knew that wasn't the real me. When I got back to the outfield, I finally stopped quaking and caught a drive, just off the left field fence. Now I was back in my rhythm.

On deck just before my first Major League at-bat. Washington vs. Boston. R.F.K. Memorial Stadium. May 15, 1961

It took a couple of innings, but I was back by the third time up. With things back to normal, my focus was on timing. The ball looked like any other ball. So I picked a good pitch and had a good swing. That swing resulted in my first big-league hit–a single.

Pitcher Billy Muffett threw the ball to first base eight straight times, and finally I took off for second. When the dust cleared, I had stolen my first base in the big leagues, and we won the doubleheader. I don't know how many fans attended, but I signed autographs for more than an hour. I learned that the big league is more than a bat and a ball.

Nothing up to that point could compare to that game. All I can tell you is that I felt good, and I thank God. We won both games, and I was one happy camper! I was always pleased to be a Major Leaguer. It was a joy to share a career with so many people–fans and players alike. The Major Leagues–the name itself means the best.

MY TIME AT BAT — A STORY OF PERSEVERANCE

THE HOUSE THAT RUTH BUILT

In 1961, I had first-hand experience with the home run duel between Mickey Mantle and Roger Maris. Seemingly, everyone was pulling for Mickey to break The Babe's long-standing season home run record. I don't remember the exact number of home runs they each hit against us, but it seemed as if it were six or seven apiece. That's a rack of home runs to get against one team.

My rookie season was like a fairy tale. I'll never forget my first visit to Yankee Stadium. I was so excited to be going there. Seeing so many Yankee games, not to mention the World Series, on television, I felt as if I had been there many times before. When I stepped foot on Yankee ground, I wanted to act like it was just another place, but in my heart I knew differently. This is a place where I had dreamed about being but didn't really know if I would get there. This was, after all, the great Yankee Stadium–"the house that Ruth built."

Then the dressing room was where my hero, Jackie Robinson, had been. He played for the Dodgers, but he played so many games against the Yankees, including in the World Series. Just that thought made me feel special. When I saw my name on my very own locker stall, I had another thrill. I got dressed and went to the dugout. The Yankees were taking batting practice, and right away I recognized the players by their numbers and from seeing them on TV.

Then I walked over to the batting cage, and to my surprise, they said, "Chuck," and came over to shake my hand. I tried to be real cool and spoke to everyone who greeted me. Again I was thrilled. When it was time for our batting practice, I went to the outfield to shag balls for the extra guys–those who weren't in the lineup that game–who hit first.

I went straight to center field and read the names on the backboards: Babe Ruth, Lou Gehrig, Joe DiMaggio. I was impressed, to say the least. I was also thrilled to be there to experience the feeling. But I had to ready myself for what I was there for: to be a factor in helping our team win. We had a two-game series, and we won both games with a very good Yankee team by scores of 3-2, then 8-7. Since I had been there, we had won all four games. When we went to Baltimore for a two-game series, we lost both

On Stage at the Show

games by scores of 4-2 and 4-3. No place was like New York, and no team was like the Yankees in 1961.

During my first at-bat in Yankee Stadium, I was about to get into the batter's box when Yogi Berra, the great Yankee catcher, said, "Hi, Chuck. How's your family? How are things going? I see where you have been doing very well." I couldn't believe what I was hearing! So I stepped out of the batter's box, reached down and got some dirt. I then told Yogi, "Please don't talk to me. I've got enough problems with Whitey Ford (a Hall of Fame pitcher). I don't need any more." We laughed, and so did the umpire. He didn't say anything else.

MOMMA'S GAME

Checo often tells a story about my first home run against the Yankees. It was my first time playing against them, August 13, 1961. My mother, brothers and sister Ellen were attending the game. It was the first time my mother saw me play in the Major Leagues. "Momma," I said, "I'm gonna hit

My homerun against Yankee pitcher Jim Bouton. R.F.K. Memorial Stadium, May 6, 1964

a home run for you today." I was somewhat surprised when I made good on my promise in the first inning. It was the leadoff home run. Checo said, "That nigga' is baaaad"–you have to know Checo to appreciate that comment.

Momma's home run was hit off pitcher Bud Daley. I later hit a home run off Hall of Fame Yankee pitcher Whitey Ford, on August 6, 1963, in the first inning. I was batting third, and there were two outs…oh, how sweet it was. And on August 6, 1964, I hit two home runs in one game against the Yankees: one off Jim Bouton in the first inning and the other in the third inning, facing Stan Williams.

In any event, "Momma's game" was a lot of fun and a fond memory that I cherish. In the next nine seasons, up until the Senators moved to Texas and became the Rangers, no other Senator hit more than .300. So that makes me the last Senator to hit more than .300. I am looking forward to getting another team in D.C. and seeing that record demolished. That's what life is about–doing the best you can do. You may pass someone up, but then someone surpasses you. Records are made to be broken.

'GAME OF THE WEEK'

As a Rookie, I got my first taste of fame. We played the Chicago White Sox, and the game was on "Game of the Week," a nationally televised baseball show. It was to us what "Monday Night Football" is to the NFL today. I was with the Senators then. The stage was set, and now it was time to show the nation what I was all about. We were playing in Chicago, and the White Sox had a good team with a really good pitching staff, good defense and lots of speed.

That particular Saturday, I was so happy because I knew my mother and all of Rocky Mount, North Carolina, would be watching. Washington was seldom, if ever, on "Game of the Week." But this night was different.

Juan Pizzaro, a very hard-throwing, left-handed pitcher, was on the mound. In the seventh inning, the White Sox were leading 3-2, and I was up. I hit a home run to lead off the inning. My home run tied the game. I felt as if I were on cloud nine. I kind of floated around the bases. It felt so good that I don't remember my feet touching the ground. I ran around the

On Stage at the Show

bases as if I hit forty-five homeruns a year. I knew that not only was Rocky Mount watching, but the entire nation was watching.

So many people told me they saw my home run. Even some of my college teammates saw it. This was one of my most cherished moments. I think the White Sox won that game. "Game of the Week" always aired on Saturdays, and that meant a lot of people saw me do my thing. What a thrill it was! There are times when you really want to show that you are a true player who can do the things that make a person stand out. "Game of the Week" gives you that feeling. Thank you, television. You helped to provide me with one of my greatest moments.

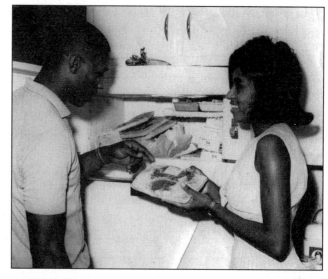
Bunny and I in our first D.C. apartment. I loved to eat! 1961

THE BEGINNING OF A BEAUTIFUL RELATIONSHIP

By the way, I started playing golf when the team had a golf outing. I asked the other black players to come along, and they said, "We don't play golf." I responded, "I don't, either."

I went along since it was a team event—just to hang out with the guys. When I got there, some of the players invited me to play—partially because they wanted to include me, but mainly because I was a braggart and they knew I didn't play golf. I said, "I don't play golf, and I don't have any clubs." "The club will take care of that," they responded. Whatever I said I lacked they said would be provided for me. So I ran out of excuses.

Unlike most beginners, I always hit the ball and never whipped it. Now, I wasn't hitting the ball where it was supposed to be; nevertheless, I would

51

hit it–and I could hit it hard and far. We were playing in pairs, hitting alternating shots.

I was paired with the 1948 U.S. Open Champion, Lew Worsham. On one hole, we had a fifty-foot putt–hard breaking. Lew told me to hit the ball one way; it was like telling me to hit south when it looked as though you should hit east. "Trust me," he insisted. So I listened to him, putt the ball as he had instructed, and to my surprise, it went in the hole. We won the tournament. I had a new perspective on golf.

I appreciated the skill and knowledge necessary to play this game. My friend Sam Lacy, Hall of Fame sports writer of *The Afro-American Newspaper*, gave me my first full set of clubs, and I started practicing and playing regularly. To this day, I play as much as I can. I'd worked my handicap down to two, but now it's back up to ten. I can still hit decently.

One of my biggest thrills on the golf course was playing golf with Jackie Robinson. I don't remember how, or who set it up, but there was a foursome, and I was really a beginner, but Jackie had no problem in taking up $15. I was so thrilled that it was a high in my life. I know how it feels to be in the presence of your hero. So many fans have told me I was their hero. I never take it lightly because I know the feeling. I still get requests for autographs and would like to have more requests for card shows or speaking engagements. I don't think I would never get tired of telling people that I am still proud to have played for eleven years.

BUSINESS TYCOON

After my rookie season, I became an insurance agent and opened Chuck Hinton Insurance Agency. I was not surprised that I passed the exam to become an agent the first time I took it. When most people want something bad enough, they will do whatever it takes to get it.

We focused mainly on automobile insurance. But we also wrote home and life insurance policies. A lot of people attended the star-studded grand opening of our first office. We had cake, champagne and a few other goodies and souvenirs. It was a lot of fun.

The next year, we had expanded into three other locations around the D.C. area. The funny thing about it was that my partner would rent an air-

On Stage at the Show

plane to advertise the company. The plane flew over and around D.C. Stadium during games with the banner saying, "Chuck Hinton Insurance Agency 332-7211."

We also promoted and advertised using billboards and radio spots. Business was going well. We were really on a roll because we were helping a lot of people get insurance who were turned down by most agencies because of their driving records. Although no one in the front office has ever told me so, I am sure the planes flying around the stadium every other Sunday eventually got me traded from Washington.

LOOKING EVERY BIT the prosperous businessman, Chuck Hinton glimpses the passing parade from outside his offices.

When I was later traded to Cleveland, I had to give the business up, but it was a great experience. Chuck Hinton Insurance Agency was big in and around the Washington, D.C. area.

D.C.–DEVOTED CITY

The 1962 spring training went well. As the team headed north to open the season, everyone was in shape and ready for the bell to ring. Washington always opened the season a day earlier than the other teams. The president of the United States would throw the first ball.

I can't put into words the feeling of opening day in D.C. Banners were waving, the stadium was packed, and the good-natured fans of D.C. were cheering.

D.C. had the best fans, although the team really wasn't very good. However, no one could accuse the team of not hustling. We were always fighting at D.C. Stadium. Later that stadium would be renamed RFK.

MY TIME AT BAT — A STORY OF PERSEVERANCE

President John F. Kennedy and Senators' president Pete Quesada at Griffith Stadium on the Expansion Senators' first Opening Day. 1961

Because I had such great experiences there, I was honored to be inducted into The Washington, D.C. Hall of Stars at RFK in 1984.

I started in the opening game that season but was in and out of the lineup for three weeks. George Case threatened to send me back to the Minor League because my hitting was off. *Off* was an understatement; I was hitting .197 and stinking up the place. I reassured him that if he would tell the powers-that-be to put me in the lineup every day for one week, I would take care of the rest. My wish was granted. I held true to my word, and when the season ended, I had hit .310, fourth in the American League, just behind Mickey Mantle.

ON THE AIR

In 1962, I also started hosting a fifteen-minute sports radio show Monday through Friday on WUST. I mostly reported sports scores and who would be playing. I reported on all major sports, including horseracing and golf. Whenever we won a game, I was real happy to report on what happened in that game. When we lost, I told the score and went on to something else. I don't remember interviewing anyone on the show. I didn't have guests because it was a cheap show—I was paid $25 per show. Anyway, by the time they added in commercials, I didn't have time to do much. But I had a really good time doing the show.

When I later took a trip to Europe to teach baseball, I taped the shows for the time I was to be away. I even gave a clinic to the listeners on how to play every position, which I thought was my best work on the air. Very seldom do you get free advice from a Major League player. When I returned

On Stage at the Show

from Europe, I spoke a little Spanish—and I do mean a little. In fact, que pasa, buenas noches, gracias and ¿cómo está usted? was the extent of my Spanish.

When we went on the road, I did the show by telephone, live and in living color. My show was on in the early evening, so I was able to talk about a lot of things that happened earlier in the day.

My show was sponsored by a beer company. At the time, I thought nothing of it. If I had the same chance today, I would pass. I would not want to be associated with a beer company.

EUROPEAN TOUR

After my 1962 season, I was asked to go to Europe for a baseball

I am having a ball at R.F.K. Stadium. Norm Seiburn of Kansas City also pictured. 1962

clinic being held at the military base in Madrid, Spain. The clinic was for five days. However, the trip lasted two weeks. As a reward, I could make stops in Barcelona, Spain; Berlin, Wiesbaden and Frankfurt, Germany; Paris and Rome.

I was the first black player to make that trip as part of the State Department's Goodwill Tour. At the clinic, we taught the game of baseball to Spanish kids and coaches. The people were receptive and friendly. There were more than one hundred fifty participants every day. We were surprised by the amount of interest the clinic fostered because at that time, baseball wasn't popular overseas, with the exception of a few countries such as Japan and those in Latin America. There were only three of us players on the tour.

I enjoyed the clinic and saw many beautiful sites. It snowed in Madrid, which I believe is uncommon because the people were watering the snow

MY TIME AT BAT — A STORY OF PERSEVERANCE

CHUCK TAKES time out from his insurance duties to autograph an 'insurance policy' of a different type—one that will guarantee him a fat salary with the Nats in 1964. Presiding at the signing is George Selkirk, general manager of the Senators.

like it was grass. Of course, the snow then became ice. In Spain, I bought my wife a bottle of perfume. Unto this day, she uses no other fragrance.

During this time, Berlin was war-torn. The remains of buildings were piled up all over the city–the result of the barrage of allied bombs. The Berlin wall, which divided East and West Germany, was still standing. We were given a short tour behind the wall. It was interesting to see the site, which was on the news daily. It was moving to be standing at a line that people gave their lives to cross.

At that time, it was almost February, and I had not signed my contract for the 1963 Major League season. So I used that as an excuse to cut my trip short. I missed out on Paris and Rome. It was a once-in-a-lifetime trip, but the truth be told, I was missing my wife and two children. And I can honestly say I've never regretted coming home early.

For one thing, we were in Frankfurt, and up until that time, I had never been in weather that cold. I might have stayed if the weather were pleasing. But when you get homesick, nothing seems to go right. I still haven't seen Paris or Rome, but you don't miss what you haven't seen.

Chapter Eight

Many Years to Come

I was back in the United States, and oh, what a wonderful feeling it was to be listed among such baseball greats as Mickey Mantle. By this time, I already had so many memorable moments in the Major Leagues. But I was just getting started. I had nine more memory-making years ahead of me in the Major Leagues. However, as you're about to find out, not all of them were shining moments.

1963–THE YEAR OF THE BEAN

The most memorable moment of the following season was not a highlight of my career. It was September 5, 1963, and we were playing the Yankees in New York. At that time in the league, we didn't wear protective helmets while at bat. We wore a little plastic liner inside our caps. It covered the temple area but not the ears.

The first pitch Ralph Terry threw me was a curve ball. It started at me but curved at home plate. I had a good swing at it, but I missed it. The next pitch was a fastball. I assumed it would curve off, but it didn't. I ducked, but

MY TIME AT BAT — A STORY OF PERSEVERANCE

With the Washington Senators 1963

being that it was a fastball, I didn't duck fast enough. That was my first time being hit any place even *near* my head.

They carried me off the field. I never lost consciousness but was rushed to the hospital with a concussion. My sister Doris, who lived in New York, was at that game. She rode with me in the ambulance, crying all the way. Ralph came by the hospital to see me and apologized for the bean, assuring me that it was an accident. That was a kind gesture. However, it was my fault. I should have gotten out of the way. We later became teammates in Cleveland.

Due to the concussion, I was out for two weeks and probably should not have played any more that season. I didn't let anyone know I was seeing double. That went on for about a week. I wanted to play because I had to prove to myself that I was not afraid of pitches. I did overcome my fear–so much so that I almost got beaned again because I didn't duck for one of the two balls I was seeing. I only got four hits the rest of that season. I was seeing two balls but never hit the real one.

To this day, I have a constant ring and diminished hearing in my left ear because of being hit. It was just an occupational hazard. The next season, protective helmets were the norm in the league.

1964–AN ALL-STAR YEAR

The next season, I was able to see straight again and even achieved some highlights of my baseball career. The players voted me into the 1964 All-Star Game (unlike some of the other league leaders, who were *placed* on the team). I was the first expansion Senator to be voted into the All-Star Game.

Many Years to Come

As it turns out, left fielder Harmon Killebrew started the game. Since he hit three for four, they left him in the game.

I didn't get in until the bottom of the ninth inning. I really should have been inserted earlier, but what can you do? The game was tied when I finally got to play outfield. Willie Mays hit a drive out to me. I fielded the ball and threw it to the shortstop. That was a single. They walked the next batter. Then Johnny Callison hit the home run that gave the National League the victory. Had we gone to the tenth inning, I would have been next at bat. Oh well, sometimes that's the way the cookie crumbles.

Still, being an All-Star with some of the greatest players the world has ever known was an outstanding experience I am blessed to have had. I was most excited to see Willie Mays for the first time. This was because I was in the American League, and he was in the National League. Inter-league play during the regular season didn't start until the year 2000. I usually got to see players from other teams during spring training. However, the Senators trained in Florida, and his team, the Giants, trained in Arizona. Therefore, our paths never crossed until the All-Star Game.

He gave me a "Say, Hey" in the batting cage. I was happy to greet him but more looking forward to seeing him play. It was a predicament because I wanted to see him at his best, but I didn't want the American League team to lose—although at that time, the National League always won the All-Star Games. I considered him to be the best all-around player in baseball—by far. The way he played in that game was unbelievable. Once I saw him play, my opinion was solidified: He was the greatest player baseball had ever known, primarily because he could do everything. He could beat you with his batting, his throwing arm, his fielding and his speed on the bases. Everything he did, he did exceptionally well. There aren't many players who can do that. He is one of the only players to have hit more than 600 home runs—surpassed only by Hank Aaron and Babe Ruth.

I soon had the opportunity to get closer to Willie Mays. In 1964, I was traded to Cleveland for Woody Held and Bob Chance. It was a good move for both teams. Since the San Francisco Giants trained in Phoenix and Cleveland trained in Tucson, I got a chance to see Willie Mays quite a bit, and we often played golf together.

MY TIME AT BAT — A STORY OF PERSEVERANCE

All-Star Game 35
Shea Stadium, New York
July 7, 1964
NL, 7-4

				R	H	E
AL	100	002	100	4	9	1
NL	000	210	004	7	8	0

MVP: Johnny Callison, PHI

Pitchers: (4), Short (6), Farrell (7), MARICHAL (9)
Home Runs: B. Williams-N, Boyer-N, Callison-N
Attendance: 50,850

The National League rallied for four runs in the bottom of the ninth to win. Willie Mays led off with a walk and stole second. Orlando Cepeda drove in Mays to tie the game and went to second on Joe Pepitone's throwing error. After Johnny Edwards was intentionally walked, Johnny Callison homered over the right-field wall.

Rosters

American League	National League
Bob Allison	Hank Aaron
Luis Aparicio*	Ken Boyer
Eddie Bressoud+	Jim Bunning
Dean Chance	Smoky Burgess+
Rocky Colavito	Johnny Callison
Whitey Ford+	Leo Cardenas
Bill Freehan+	Orlando Cepeda
Jim Fregosi	Roberto Clemente
Jimmie Hall	Don Drysdale
Chuck Hinton	Johnny Edwards
Elston Howard	Dick Ellsworth+
Al Kaline*	Turk Farrell
Harmon Killebrew	Curt Flood
Jack Kralick+	Dick Groat
Jerry Lumpe+	Ron Hunt
Frank Malzone+	Sandy Koufax+
Mickey Mantle	Juan Marichal
Tony Oliva	Willie Mays
Camilo Pascual	Bill Mazeroski+
Joe Pepitone	Ron Santo+
Gary Peters+	Chris Short
Juan Pizarro+	Willie Stargell
Dick Radatz	Joe Torre
Bobby Richardson	Bill White
Brooks Robinson	Billy Williams
Norm Siebern	
John Wyatt	

*Named to team but replaced due to injury
+Did not enter game

Many Years to Come

Manager Mickey Vernon of the Senators (right) looks over some of the silver three of his players received last night at a meeting of the Grandstand Managers of Alexandria. Dave Stenhouse (left), was voted most valuable pitcher; Chuck Hinton (center), most valuable player, and Tom Cheney (right) was picked for outstanding achievement. Cheney set a major league record with 21 strikeouts against the Orioles recently.—Star Staff Photo.

In the Major Leagues, you learn that baseball is a business, and you may be traded at any time. Only a small number of players stay with one team throughout their careers. So it's not a big deal to be traded. Regardless, unless you had been playing for ten years, you had no choice where you were traded.

I was with Washington from 1961-64. I led the team in batting three out of the four seasons. I led the team in stolen bases and triples all four years. I led the team in doubles two years and tied one year, 1963, with Eddie Brinkman. I led the team in base hits in 1962, 1963 and 1964. I ended up being in Cleveland twice: 1965-67 and 1969-71.

THE CLEVELAND INDIANS

Cleveland was a great place to play, although it was freezing cold. Early and late in the season in Old Municipal Stadium, the winds would come up

MY TIME AT BAT — A STORY OF PERSEVERANCE

from Lake Erie and shoot right through you. Good, young talent was plentiful, but we never really put it all together. We did finish second to the Orioles in 1966. Of all the teams I played with, that was the best finish. During my six years in Cleveland, I played every position except pitcher.

As in D.C., opening day in Cleveland was a thrill. The fans were excited, and the stadium was packed. There were so many thrills on a daily basis. Catching the last out of Sunny Siebert's no-hit/no-run game against the Senators was one of them.

Another was during a promotional night at Municipal Stadium in front of 66,000 fans. It started out unfortunate. I made an error when the ball rolled between my legs after hitting my glove. This led to Minnesota scoring the tying run in the ninth inning. Unless you've heard 66,000 people boo, you haven't heard booing. In the top of the tenth inning, I was on deck when we made the last out. When I headed out for left field, the boos were still in full force. When we went back to the dugout, I was the first hitter, and the boos started again when I went to the plate.

I'll never forget it. Al Worthington was pitching. He was tough to hit and threw a mean slider. Usually, I was so focused that I would not hear the crowd, but you can't shut out 66,000 people. Worthington was already tough enough, but now he was getting extra help from our angry fans. The count was one ball and one strike when I hit a home run to win the game. Now, unless you've heard 66,000 people cheer, you haven't heard cheering!

With the Cleveland Indians 1965

I hit my first and only grand slam home run against Washington pitcher Ron Kline. It was at D.C. Stadium on May 5, 1965. The Washington fans had mixed emotions. They wanted me to do well, but fans never want their team to lose. I

Many Years to Come

played this game like I did any other. Sometimes you hear about players having grudges against their former teams. I didn't play any harder against Washington because I was traded. In any event, it was a great moment for me.

I MISSED ANOTHER ONE

The season was almost over when our third child, Kimberly Elise, was born. Once again, I was out of town. We almost lost Kim. She contracted jaundice shortly after being born and had to stay in an incubator for a month. When I got home, I went to the hospital to check on her every day. Shortly before my mother passed away, she visited Kim in the hospital and said to me, "C, you finally have a child that looks just like you."

Kim was really sick. She was being fed intravenously through a tube inserted into her head. But she didn't look sick; she looked like a fat, healthy baby. Kim was full of life and always smiling. She has always been a lot like me–and very smart. She was reading the newspaper at three years old. When I was home, she would follow me around and never let me out of her sight. When I would go to the restroom, she would wait at the door until I came out.

My third child, Kimberly Elise Stewart. 2001

Today, Kimberly's husband, Derwin Stewart, is the founder and president of Pneuma Life Publishing Inc., one of the largest African-American-owned Christian publishing companies in the country. Together, they are quite a team. Kimberly also heads up the imprint Christian Living Books Inc.

My Time at Bat — A Story of Perseverance

PART OF THE TRIBE

During my six seasons with the Cleveland Indians, transportation was interesting and, at times, challenging. To reach Hopkins International Airport there, you had to cross a very active railroad track. The long freight train made many players miss their flights. Sometimes the train took twenty minutes or more to cross. If you missed the team's chartered flight, you were on your own. That meant you had to pay for the next flight out to make the game. Sometimes, the traveling secretary would leave your ticket if he was aware that you didn't make the flight. However, that was not always the case. If your ticket was not left for you, you had to handle the arrangements yourself.

Sometimes, four of us players would carpool to the airport. Believe me, we allowed plenty of time for the train to pass, and we would make the flight. Even today, I refuse to be late. Perhaps that train remains ever in my mind. People understand that things happen, but in most cases, a person is late because he didn't allow enough time for the inevitable "things" that come up.

Spring Training, Tucson, AZ. 1966

I always consider other people's time. Their time is as valuable as yours. Don't keep people waiting. Plan ahead to be there on time. In everyday life, everything has a starting and ending time. Make it a habit to do what you said you would do. After all, people like to know they can depend on you. And you want people to trust your word. In professional baseball, you are fined for being late—especially if you have been late a couple of times.

To this day, I visit Cleveland each year, but the

freight train problem no longer exists. An overpass has been built at the train track.

ANGELS IN THE OUTFIELD

At the end of spring training in 1968, I was traded again, this time to California for Jose Cardanal. Being in and out of the lineup was not good for me. I had the worst year of my career as a hitter: 267 AB, 52 H, 7 HR, 23 RBIs and a .195 average. I blame the slump mainly on not playing regularly enough. However, during that time, I did play a lot of golf—at least three or four times a week—and met a few movie stars. One of them, Carmen Mitchell, and I would play golf together all the time. He was the first golfer I saw who had all woods. It was a strange sight to see a player hit a wood out of a green side bunker. Hey, different strokes…

I loved the weather in California, but the Angels didn't win many games. Nonetheless, I enjoyed my time there and made lifelong friendships, which is true for each team I was on.

I got game-winning hits and made game-winning defensive plays, but I was glad when the season was over. I was looking forward to a fresh start. I really worked hard during the off-season because I wasn't pleased with my performance that season.

At the end of the 1969 spring training, I was traded back to Cleveland for Lou Johnson.

Once back in a regular lineup, I had my highest batting average ever at the end of a Major League season, .318. For the next three seasons, we chased the Orioles, Yankees and Twins, but they had strong teams. We finished third, fourth and fifth.

I distinctly remember another game against Washington, on August 8, 1970. The score was tied 2-2 in the top of the ninth with two outs. Ray Fosse, our catcher, hit a double. Washington's manager, Ted Williams, went to the mound to talk to the pitcher, Darold Knowles. Knowing the situation, I am sure they were discussing whether they would pitch *to* me or *around* me, since first base was open. I was announced as a pinch hitter. Because there were two outs, I expected them to walk me. However, Knowles decided to pitch to me. By the time Ted got back to the dugout, I had hit a home run to win the game 4-2.

THREE FOR FOUR

The home run was a highlight in my career. But I had missed another highlight in my personal life–the birth of my last child, Tiffany Ermette, on July 19. She looked just like my sister Ruth. She was the baby all the way. She kept her bottle until she was in first grade. It got to the point where she was old enough to fill her own bottle. When she visited Bunny's aunt Lula in Brooklyn, she even went to the corner store and bought her own milk.

My fourth child, Tiffany Ermette Salaberrios. 1995

Tiffany was a little trooper, a safety patrol who manned her corner, rain, sleet or snow. She was always dramatic, our little movie star. Tiffany was also studious. She was valedictorian in junior high school and senior class president in high school. She left Howard University her junior year to attend the National Conservatory of Dramatic Arts. She now lives in New York with her husband, Dimas Salaberrios, where she is pursuing her dream of being an actress. They are the founders of Missionary Soldiers, a nonprofit organization committed to sharing the Gospel.

WHAT MATTERS MOST

Although I missed three out of four of my children's births because I was playing baseball–quite a record–I never lost sight of what has always mattered most to me: my family. I spoiled every one of my children. We had such fun as a family.

My kids were too young to remember my playing days; they learned that Dad was a good baseball player. However, more than that they learned more about the person I really am. No matter what games we played together, I never *let* them win. They had to beat me with their skill, talent or thinking. They learned lessons. For in life, nobody gives you anything. You have to earn it.

Even today, we are a close family. We are all born-again Christians, and I am proud to have the family that God has given me. We pray together, and we'll always stay together. Bunny is a wonderful mother who always recognized the individual interests and talents in each of our children and then cultivated and nurtured them. We all adore her and have agreed that she is *an excellent person.*

To show some of my abounding appreciation, I held a surprise birthday party for Bunny in 1963. I had told all of the players on the Senators about the party and that I wanted them to come and help celebrate. I had family and friends help prepare the food and make sure they were at my house an hour after the game. Bunny's birthday is June 11, and in Washington, it is hot that time of year. I don't know how all those people got in the basement and were so quiet that when we got home, Bunny never heard or suspected what was going on. That is, she never told me if she knew.

Bunny and I out on the town in New York. 1964

Not only were all the teammates and their wives there, but the manager, the coaches, their wives, and lots of friends and relatives were there as well. She was so outdone when I told her I wanted her to go with me to

My Time at Bat — A Story of Perseverance

Beautiful Bunny. 1979

the basement to check on something. When she cut on the light and they all shouted, "Surprise! Happy Birthday!" it frightened her at first. But she gathered herself and began to shed tears of joy. The food was on time, the drinks were flowing and the lies got bigger. We had a great time, and I guess everyone went home around 3 A.M. To this day, when I see former teammates, black and white, they talk about that party.

Bunny has been the anchor of my life, my one and only true love. She will disarm you with her incredible sweetness and her angelic voice. I have yet to meet anyone with her combination of intelligence, breathtaking beauty, charm, kindness and compassion. We've weathered some storms in life, and Bunny has handled them all with grace and strength. I have the greatest respect for her.

My wife is a queen *and* a saint, with a heart of gold. She goes to hospitals to pray for the sick and shares the love of Jesus on the streets of D.C. A genuine person, Bunny never ceases to amaze me. I am at a loss for words to express the depth of my appreciation for her. I would not be the man I am today had she not embraced me with her unfailing devotion and unconditional love.

Bunny is truly, truly precious—my priceless jewel, my delicate flower. I love her more with each passing year. We pray together each morning. If I am out of town, then we pray over the telephone. We have a wonderful, fulfilling marriage. God has blessed me with Bunny, a gift from heaven.

Chapter Nine

More Memorable Moments

As I think back on my years in the Major Leagues, so many stories stand out in my mind. Some of them taught me and others lessons; others made me proud; many to this day make me laugh hysterically when I think about them.

One thing I–or should I say, the opposing pitcher–learned from experience is it doesn't pay to talk that much about another player because he doesn't forget what you said. It could come back to haunt you. Such was the case with me in 1962 in Minnesota against the Twins' relief pitcher, Ray Moore. In the ninth inning of a game, the Senators had one out with runners on first and third bases–in scoring position–and Minnesota was leading by one run. Moore struck out Chuck Cottier, and I was up to bat next.

What made the game important to me was the fact that I would be going in to catch if we tied the game. Although it had been quite some time since I had been a catcher, I was elated to be called in to play. So my desire to get a hit was greater than usual. Ray threw me some heat. I was crushed when he got the best of me–striking me out and ending the game. The Minnesota newspaper quoted Ray as saying, "I just smoked Cottier and

My Time at Bat — A Story of Perseverance

With the Washington Senators 1964

Hinton away." I say Ray *was quoted* because you can never be one hundred percent sure that everything you read in the paper is accurate. I really never forgot that quote. More than anything, I didn't forget the way things turned out to end that game.

Three weeks later, the Minnesota Twins came to Washington for a three-game series. One night, I was not in the starting lineup but went in to pinch hit in the eighth inning. I was walked, and I scored to tie the game 3-3. I stayed in the game as an outfielder, and neither team scored in the ninth inning.

We got them out without scoring in the top of the tenth inning. In our half of that inning, we had runners on first and second bases with two outs. Ray Moore was called to pitch to me. For those weeks since the last Minnesota game, all I could see was that quote. I was so fired up that I really had to calm myself down because I was full of hate, and that is not good. By the time he finished his warm-up pitches, I had calmed down and had become focused.

I was looking for a fastball, and sure enough, I got just one. I don't remember the count, but the ball was so big to me. I crushed it over the fence into the bull pen for a three-run home run. No, I did not bad mouth him in the paper. No quote was necessary. I had gotten my pay back.

Something else I learned from experience is a pitcher will go to any lengths to intimidate you, even when he is your friend. It was no picnic facing black pitchers because you were friends with them and you might hang out together. However, when it came to the game, friendship was left outside the park. Earl Wilson was with Boston, then Detroit. We would hang

More Memorable Moments

out together when one of us was in the other's city. We were the best of friends. He threw as hard as any pitcher in the league.

Pitchers often throw certain pitches to intimidate you. You can't ever allow that to happen. If you are overly concerned about getting hit, you can't ever hit the ball. When you show fear, the intimidation has worked and will continue until you overcome the fear. Those are the times at which you must "take your licking and keep on ticking."

VERY FUNNY

On a lighter note, many players kept a sense of humor, even when things didn't go their way. One time was when I was playing with Cleveland, and the left-fielder, Leon Wagner, went back to the fence and reached up for a fly ball. The ball hit the side of his glove and bounced over the fence in Cleveland Municipal Stadium for a home run. When we got to the dugout, the starting pitcher told Wags that he should have caught the ball. Leon told him, "Since you are so good, why did you let him hit the ball to me in the first place?" Everybody cracked up.

I remember another funny situation when I was with Cleveland. Frank Robinson, who was on the opposing team, the Orioles, hit a pitch off Luis Tiant over the left field stands at Memorial Stadium in Baltimore. The hit was loud, and it looked like the ball was going into the upper deck. But it sailed over the bleachers and clear out of the stadium. When we made our third out and went to the dugout, Gary Bell, another pitcher for Cleveland, went over to Luis and asked him, "How did you hold the ball? Cross seam or what?" Frank was the only player to have ever hit one out of that stadium.

Also when I was with Cleveland, Lee Strange was pitching for us against Washington. Frank Howard, a Washington outfielder, hit a line drive that hit Lee on his upper arm. The ball went a few feet from him, and he pounced on it and made the throw to first base for the third out. He walked to the dugout, and as soon as he hit the bottom step, he passed out. We all laughed hysterically. He soon recovered and went on to win the game.

Another time, when I was with Cleveland, Cleveland third baseman Greg Nettles was facing pitcher Darold Knowles. Both of them were left-handed. After a ball was thrown at his head, Greg tried to throw the bat at

MY TIME AT BAT — A STORY OF PERSEVERANCE

the pitcher. Instead the bat went to first base, where Washington's Frank Howard was playing. Frank was called the gentle giant because he was 6'7" and 350 pounds. Everyone from our dugout and bull pen ran out to go help Greg out. As you know, that is a baseball custom. But Frank stood right in front of our dugout with his arms outstretched and yelled, "Stop! We are even!" The funny thing was that everyone froze right in his tracks, including me. We all tipped–as opposed to charged–to the infield, where nothing took place. Frank took the fight out of everyone.

When I was playing for Washington, I was known for my speed. Paul Blair, a great outfielder for the Baltimore Orioles, sure learned that the hard way. I hit a single to center field and rounded first base really fast. I faked as if I were going back to first base. So Paul made a great throw to first base. As soon as he released the ball, I simply trotted to second base. It was a hard lesson to learn and quite embarrassing. But Paul never let it happen again.

I also recall a humorous moment with an old Army teammate. John Wyatt was a hard-throwing relief pitcher for Kansas City and talked a lot of trash. We had been in the service together, stationed at Fort Bragg. We both played on the All Post team. There were many Army teams, but this one had the best players and represented the third Army Division in the division tournaments. We were the best of friends. When in Kansas City or Washington, we would have dinner together after each game.

100th Career Homerun against pitcher Marcel Lachemann. Cleveland vs. Oakland. Cleveland Memorial Memorial Stadium. 1970

We faced each other many times. However, one particular game, for about five straight times, he got me out. And if I popped up or even flied out, he would make it his business to tell me to go sit down and get some water. I told him that not only was I going to hit a tater (home run), I was going to embarrass him also. Furthermore, I said, it won't be pretty.

More Memorable Moments

With a man on first, it was my turn to bat again. When I hit the ball, I knew it was gone. I hit a home run off him. I stood at the plate, then slowly put my bat to my shoulder like a shotgun and began to shoot him all the way to first base before throwing the bat down. "Bang, bang...told you I would get you...bang, bang." Being that we were old Army buddies, it was the most appropriate gesture I could make toward him. He lowered his head in laughter. We had a great time with that. Those kinds of moments were priceless.

OTHER HOME RUN HIGHLIGHTS

Over the years, my home runs provided other memorable moments in my career. One was when Cleveland was playing in Boston. Seldom do you win in extra innings on the road because the home team has the last at-bat. But this time was different. We were in the twelfth inning, with two runners on base and two outs. I was up to bat, and Don McMahon was the pitcher for Boston. He threw me a slider that hung a little, and I hit a home run over the Green Monster—the nickname for the notorious left field fence in Boston.

We were on our way to the bus after the game when Gabe Paul, our general manager, called me over and congratulated me on the homer. He put some money in my hand and said, "Have a good dinner." What a surprise. Even some of my teammates still don't believe it happened. I almost passed out when I saw three twenty dollar bills. Indeed I had a *very* good dinner, just as he requested.

In another instance, Cleveland was the opposing team. When Cleveland's pitcher that game, Luis Tiant, came to the big league, he won his first four games. Luis had just beaten the Yankees when he came to Washington to play us. We were in the eighth inning, and Cleveland was leading 3-1. Things were going Luis' way, and he was well on his way to another win. We had two outs, with runners on first and second. I got a pitch that I couldn't believe. It was a moment you live for. I hit a home run, and we got them out in the ninth inning for the 4-3 win. Luis got his first loss in the Capital City. Everybody was so happy because we got a rare win.

I experienced so many home run thrills, but one of the tops on my list happened in Chicago when I was with Washington, on May 5, 1963. It was the second game of a doubleheader. In the ninth inning, the White Sox were leading 7-6. The wind was blowing in at Comiskey Park. It was a cool Sunday. We had started to rally; there were two runners on base. As I came to bat, the manager called time out. A call was made to the bull pen for none other than Hoyt Wilhelm, a Hall of Fame pitcher.

He was an excellent relief pitcher who threw nothing but knuckle balls. A knuckle ball from Wilhelm will cross your eyes. The knuckle ball weaves and zigs and zags and hops and skips. By the time it gets to the plate, it takes a huge dip that makes it almost impossible to hit. To go even further, it is almost impossible to catch. A knuckle ball's catcher had to use a mitt that was three times as large as a regular catcher's mitt.

Unless you have tried to hit or catch one, you can't really know what I am saying. I can tell you that hitting a ninety-mile-an-hour fastball is so much easier than trying to hit a knuckle ball that is thrown about fifty-five or sixty miles per hour.

After watching him warm up, I decided he would probably try to get ahead with a strike. What I saw was a knuckler that started at eye level. But by the time it got in my hitting zone, it was waist high. It was a really good pitch, and I knew I just had to hit it. Everything lit up, and I was really ready. When I made contact, I knew I had gotten all of it on the *sweet part* of my bat. And I knew it had to be out of the park. In fact, it went into the upper deck...against the wind. It was the only home run I ever hit off Wilhelm. But it was a good one. It won the game for us. I was so proud of that home run.

INSIDE-THE-PARK HOMERS

I hit two inside-the-park home runs in my career. They stand out because I had to turn on the jets (extra speed) each time to make it to home plate safely. Both of them were against the Yankees. The first was against the great Whitey Ford, a Hall of Fame left-hander. I hit a sinking line drive to center field in the first game of a doubleheader. Tom Tresh, the center fielder, attempted to make a shoestring catch. When the ball got past him, I got some extra speed from somewhere. By the time Tresh got the ball and threw it to the infielder, who in turn threw to home plate, I had slid across the plate. It was the first inside-the-park home run in what was known then as D.C. Stadium. We went on to win the game 8-5.

More Memorable Moments

The other was in Yankee Stadium against pitcher Luis Arroyo, a fine left-hander who saved a lot of games for the Yankees. This was before Yankee Stadium had its face-lift. At that time, the left center field fence was 457 feet from home plate. That was much deeper and longer than any left field fence in baseball.

I hit the ball between the left fielder and center fielder. It hit the fence and rolled away from the left fielder. There were two relay throws to get the ball in. I ran as fast as I could around the bases, again sliding safely across the plate for a home run. It felt good because when you play well against the Yankees, you have done so against the best.

WALK-OFF HOMERS

I also remember getting walk-off home runs. You have to be at home to have a walk-off home run. This is when your home run wins the game in the last inning. As soon as the ball leaves the park, most of the time, the opposing team starts walking off the field. However, they make sure you touch every base and home plate. Walk-off home runs were always special. The game is on the line. You are at home, and the fans are cheering you on. It's star time!

One that stands out in my mind is the twelfth-inning home run against Minnesota's Jim Donahue in 1962. Another was June 2, 1963, against

My first inside-the-park homerun against pitcher Whitey Ford. New York Yankees vs. Washington. July 22, 1962

My Time at Bat — A Story of Perseverance

Kansas City pitcher Dale Willis. It was the tenth inning, the game was tied at 4, and we had one batter on base and two outs.

While I was with Cleveland, I hit a few. One was on June 27, 1965, when the score was 7-7 in the fifteenth inning. Two runners were on base, and we had one out. Jim Dickson of Kansas City was the pitcher. Another was June 20, 1971, against Detroit. There were no outs. I was the lead-off hitter in the eleventh inning. Fred Scherman was the pitcher. This home run was one of the highlights of my last season.

THE STADIUMS

In all my years playing baseball, I have played in almost every state. From my experiences, I have specific memories about certain stadiums, which I would like to share with you.

Baltimore

I spent almost all my Minor League time with Baltimore. In the Major Leagues, the Orioles would pitch me mostly fastballs—and they had some hard throwers. I would joke with Earl Weaver, the manager, telling him that even my hitting .358 was not enough and that I made him the manager he became.

Baltimore would beat up on Washington big time, but we managed to beat them a few times. I used to tell Brooks Robinson I was going to hit one off his knee cap. What a joke! He was, in my opinion, the best third baseman ever to play the game. I remember Milt Pappas throwing one fastball after another. I would foul off at least eight pitches, then I'd hit a home run to straightaway center field at Memorial Stadium. I think I did well against the Orioles. I don't think I tried any harder against them because of my spending most of my Minor League career there. I just wanted to beat them because they were usually a good team. After all, performing well against the best made you the best.

Detroit

Detroit's Briggs Stadium was more of a hitter park because of its background. It was some 445 feet to center field with reachable stands in left and

More Memorable Moments

right field. The sound from the batter ball was the very best in the league. I had some fond memories there. I hit three home runs in a doubleheader. For some reason, I was hitting fourth and did hit a couple of home runs in one series. Denny McLain was having a great year. He and Sam McDowell were dueling when in a 0-0 game, he threw one hard at my head. A few pitches later, I hit one in the upper deck for a most rewarding home run.

They usually had a good team. It was a joy to play them, but it was dangerous because sometimes the fans would throw things at you in the outfield.

I also remember that Jim Bunning was a fine right-hand pitcher for the Tigers. He would release the baseball about three-quarters, almost side arm. In my first at-bat against him, he threw a curve ball that started high behind me, and all I could do was hit the dirt quick. Well the umpire was laughing and saying strike one. I jumped up, ready to argue. But, I thought, How was I to know? I was busy ducking. From that time until he went to the National League, I hit him well because I made up my mind that I would never again run or duck from a pitch he threw.

Chicago

Chicago's Comiskey Park was a good park in which to hit. However, the weather was cold and windy in April, May and September. Chicago had a good team also. They had a great pitching staff, and you had to not make any mistakes because in the late innings, they had Hoyt Wilhelm, the Hall of Fame knuckle ball pitcher, in the bull pen. At different times, they also had Eddie Fisher and Wilbert Woods—also knuckle ball pitchers.

Before the Brewers settled in Milwaukee, the White Sox would play a game or two there. Wilbert Woods got me to a 3-2 count, and I fouled off his knuckle about four or five times. Then he decided to throw me his fastball. I hit it for a home run, and that was a good feeling because seldom does a knuckle-ball pitcher throw you a fastball. It also means you have to be ready to handle another pitch. I hit a few triples in Comiskey Park. Because of the distance in left and right field, the ball at times would roll away from the outfielders. You had to be ready for each at-bat because the pitching staff really worked you over.

My Time at Bat — A Story of Perseverance

Boston

Boston's Fenway Stadium was a nightmare for me because I was not a pull hitter. But that close wall in left field was so inviting. It would take a day or two to get my swing back after leaving Fenway. One time, Earl Wilson, my buddy and a pitcher for the Red Sox, threw a pitch real close to my head. Earl could throw hard. He was 6'4." Anyway, I have no way of knowing how I got out of the way. I did get up and ask him if he was crazy or what his problem was. He simply gave me a look and grinned. At any rate, I did hit a single and gave him a piece of my mind. I did hit a few home runs in Fenway. I enjoyed it there because the park was always full and the fans were hostile to all clubs. That is fun because when you beat them, you know you've done something real good by defeating the city.

Minnesota

Minnesota's Bloomington Stadium was a great place to play because they had a good team and they would long-ball you, meaning they would hit a lot of home runs. They would beat you with speed also. As soon as you would hit a home run, they would put the distance up right away. Finding a place to eat after night games there was a problem, but the visiting clubhouse attendant made the best post-game spread in the American League. Jimmy was also one of the better-paid clubhouse attendants. Minnesota pitcher Mudcat Grant was a good friend, and we play a lot of golf together. Once Mudcat pitched a thirteen-hit shutout against our Washington team. They turned six double plays. Rich Rollin at third base nearly got his chest knocked off but made about eight plays–six with his chest.

Kansas City

Kansas City Municipal Stadium had by far the best playing field. The grass was like a putting green, and the dirt was truly Major League. It was a beautifully manicured field. Kansas City was also the first team to wear uniforms with other colors—and white shoes. Owner Charlie Finley started the trend when he had his team change uniforms before the second game of a doubleheader. Previously, all teams wore black shoes at all times, along with

More Memorable Moments

white uniforms when they were home and gray uniforms when they were away.

The uniform was no joke when this team got a bunch of young bonus players and started to beat up on you. Then they moved to Oakland, California. You could see them becoming a real team. They won the World Series three years in a row: 1971, 1972 and 1973. The talk around the league was Brooks Robinson's being hit in the face by a bad hop in Oakland. Oakland could be cold in the summertime at night.

California

California played in three different stadiums: Wrigley Field (Los Angeles) in 1961, Dodger Stadium in 1962-63 and Anaheim Big A from 1964 to present. I hit my first home run against Ron Kline at Wrigley Field, where the Angels played their first season in 1961. (I also hit my one and only grand slam against Ron Kline). At Dodger Stadium, I remember our Senators pitcher hitting one of the Angels players. Jim King, a Senators outfielder, was next at bat. Then Marv Grisson, the Angels pitcher, hit Jim with a pitch. I was the next at bat during this "bean ball fight." When I hit a long home run over the center field fence, that settled things down, and the fight was over.

A SPITTING IMAGE

All stadiums are cleaned after every game, no matter how long it takes to get ready for the next day. That means the dugouts are clean when we come to them. But shortly after we arrive, you can not tell it had ever been cleaned. Everybody is either eating sunflower seeds or spitting tobacco. By the second or third inning, the floors in the dugout are *covered* with seed shells mixed with tobacco "juice." I tell you, it is a remarkable sight. Sometimes when a push broom is near, someone would sweep the dugout. But two or three innings later, the floor would be covered again.

I was not aware of my excessive spitting until my wife asked me, "Why do you spit so much?" It must be something we players pick up. I believe we spit more than any other athlete. You don't remember when you started or how much you do it. It really is a thing you did by habit. It is also called a nervous energy.

MY TIME AT BAT — A STORY OF PERSEVERANCE

I stopped chewing tobacco about ten years ago. However, I still find myself spitting at the golf course. I guess once a spitter, always a spitter. Many people have habits. Please remember that regardless of our habits, we should think of others. Now, wouldn't it be nice if we thought of others in all we do? It's the golden rule: "Do unto others as you would have them do unto you."

Chapter Ten

An Inside-the-Park Look

I have experienced so many thrills behind-the-scenes in baseball, as well, and I want to tell you about a few of them. First of all, Major League means just that–the best of everything. Everything and everyone is there to service you. When you walk into a Major League locker room, there are three uniforms per person. All of your sweatshirts and under clothing are hanging up, clean and ready to wear. Even your shoes have been shined.

Everything is neat and in order. There are all types of food and drinks: soda, fruit drinks, milk, coffee and tea. Of course, there is beer after every game.

When you make it to the show, everyone working for the club is there to make things easy for you. The front office has a listing of homes and apartments. Some clubs will give you a car for the season. They know where you should live and not live. They advise you on every part of town.

When you get ready to go on a road trip, your bag is packed for you, including your game glove and shoes. You fly almost everywhere you go, most of the time by charter plane. That means nobody is on the plane but the team and traveling parties. Charter buses were always there to take you to and from the stadium. You have a trainer available to you 24-7, and he does a great job. (But being a big-league player, you don't get sympathy, just good service.)

For the most part, the hotels were some of the best. When you arrive, your room key is ready for you. Once you get to your room, the bell captain is called to bring your luggage. You do not have to load or unload your luggage. You are given an itinerary, informing you where to be at all times. When you check out, you tell the bell captain to come get your bag.

On some trips, you would take one of your kids or your wife or even a brother or close friend. You arranged it with the team's traveling secretary, and it was done. You had all the help you needed for any travel. Each team had a traveling secretary. His responsibility would be to pass out meal and expense money, along with the week's itinerary, make all the travel arrangements, give out paychecks, and issue stadium passes for your friends and family. By 1971, my last year in the league, we were getting $22 per day for meals on the road. If we were going on a two-week road trip, we would get the cash for the two-week period in one lump sum. It was your responsibility to eat as you pleased. It was more than enough. I don't know how much the players get today, but you can rest assured it's a lot.

Everything was done to have you ready to perform on the field. All the fields in the big league are as fine as they can be, and any time you wanted something done to the field, the ground crew would do its best to do it for you.

During my day, you took pride in being a big-leaguer, and I don't think it was a team rule but rather a tradition to wear a tie and suit or jacket. Your position in life was at the top, and you dressed the part and were glad to do it.

Everything is big-league. I would sum it up by stating, you are one of the best players in the world, so the service you get is also world-class.

The service is better with every advancement in a baseball career. Each step is a giant step, from high school to college, from college to Minor League, then every class up to the show. This is because the competition is stronger, smarter and better. Every step up carries more money, better conditions, a better front office and better travel.

An Inside-the-Park Look

As you progress, you learn to adjust to every situation, including some that may not be so favorable—such as getting used to some fields that are not in the best condition or some lights that are not up to par. It is not easy facing youngsters who can throw the ball in the 90s under some lights that appear as candlelight. Not only can some throw hard, but their control is not always the best, to say the least.

Since you had to deal with whatever conditions existed, it was best to do the best you could. After all, you were being judged on your performance, and not many times will they say the light was poor or the pitcher was wild, or give any other excuse. Production is the name of the game.

It was important to realize that playing every day was hard enough in itself; you couldn't get too high or too low. You were going to have up days and down days. But regardless of the circumstances, you could always hustle and do the little things to help win games. You made sure you didn't miss any signs that were given. If a bunt was in order, you made sure to get the ball on the ground. If a ground ball to the right side was needed to get a runner to third base, or a fly ball to the outfield to score a runner, you did everything in your power to get it done. After all, that is part of winning the game; it's what is called for in those situations that makes you a team player.

It proved to be worth it. At the end of a game, dozens of fans would be waiting for autographs—on paper, pictures, baseballs, programs, shirts, and any and everything.

Eating in the clubhouse after a game was common. It was there, and some players would sit and eat and drink beer for hours after the game. After all, it was next to impossible to find an outside place to eat after games, especially in some

1963

MY TIME AT BAT — A STORY OF PERSEVERANCE

of the cities in the Minors, as most Minor League and Major League games are played at night, besides Saturday and Sunday. In most of the cities, everything would be closed. You lived on hamburgers, hot dogs and french fries because fast-food restaurants were the only places open. The towns would close down at eight or nine o'clock, but you had to eat the best you could. When you are signed to play pro ball, no one tells you much. You learn as you go. I had always had the right food while growing up. But, maintaining a healthy diet in pro ball was not easy.

Since we went to bed late, we seldom got up for breakfast. We sometimes would have a late breakfast and go back to sleep.

Many people say pro players are spoiled and want to be pampered. Well, let me tell you, if the average person would have to learn to care for himself on the road where choices are limited, he would last for one week. There are so many other things you have to go through, such as no hot water in some of the Minor League parks. Some of the hotels we stayed in were very poor, to put it mildly.

But when your goal is to reach the show, you take a licking and keep on ticking. Your complete concentration is needed on the field. You can't afford to let these outside circumstances clog your mind. You play under terrible weather conditions, plenty of times during storms, waiting for the rain to stop so they can start the game. It's so funny sometimes to see the team stall to try and get the game called or, on the other hand, try to get the fifth inning in for a complete game. I guess most baseball people know that before a game starts, the home team has the right to call a game off. Once the game starts, however, that decision belongs to the umpire.

I spent two and a half years in the Minor League, and for the most part, I really enjoyed that time. I had a good time in the Army also. I guess you can say I made the best of what I had to do. That's pretty much how I live my life, doing the best I can with what I've got or until I can get what I want.

When I was asked how it feels to be a big-leaguer, I often said very good, but very proud probably would have been more accurate. If you can think the best of everything, with all the trimmings, that would sum it up.

Yes, you are in awe of the players you read about now. You are among them. But until you make a showing for yourself or gain respect as a player —and you know you not only belong but you, too, are a player who can be

An Inside-the-Park Look

counted on—staying in the big league is just as hard as getting there. You have to get the job done consistently, or out of there you will be.

I had so many thrills on and off the baseball field. My family and I would drive across the country to Arizona then back when the season was over in California. This is a great sight to see any time of year. The Grand Canyon is breathtaking. Only God could create it—the beauty, the details, everything is placed so that man could never have done it. The small towns, the stores, the way people dress and talk is an education in itself. What a melting pot.

There are a few states I haven't seen—but only a few. I thank God for giving me the talent to do the things I've done, to meet the people I've met, to see the places I've seen, to live the life that I have lived. I truly respect what you believe or trust, but as for me and my house, we are going to serve our Lord and Savior Jesus Christ. I will always seek first the Kingdom of God and His righteousness, and then other things will be added to me.

MEET THE PRESS

On road trips, reporters and radio and TV commentators are part of the party that travels with the team, so you get questions every day. You don't let a reporter lead you into saying anything that will hurt you in the future. You have to know what to say and keep it simple. That means if you hit a home run to win the game, sure you are happy, but you don't have to knock anyone. The reporter is sure to ask you what kind of pitch you hit. I usually said I didn't know, but I saw the pitch well, and it hit on a sweet spot on the bat. I was so lucky because it was a good pitch in a good spot. With comments such as this, you don't sound like a braggart, nor do you belittle the pitcher because you are sure to face him again and again.

You can rest assured you will pay for saying the wrong thing. Pitchers don't forget the hit that cost them the game. If a pitcher wanted to hit you, and you are trying to hit, no contest, you will be hit. The pitcher can throw the ball just behind you—waist high—and it's almost impossible to get out of the way. A hitter, of course, gets angry when a pitcher throws at his head because that can end his career, or life, for that matter. But if hitting you is what he wants to do, he can do it without going for your head.

MY TIME AT BAT — A STORY OF PERSEVERANCE

Most pitchers did not hit you, but they did come close to let you know that at any time, they may. It was a matter of pride. The pitcher had to remind you sometimes that you would get a pitch high and tight, as well as a pitch down the middle of the plate. A hitter is paid to hit, while a pitcher is paid to get you out, so what both want is professional courtesy with a little respect. As you can see, there is a lot to being a Major League player. You must also be sensitive to others doing their jobs.

In Washington, there were three newspapers: *The Washington Post*, *Evening Star* and *Daily News*. Every day they had to report the game and get their stories out for their readers. They sometimes would misquote you, but most of the time, they were kind to the players.

LEAVE NOTHING TO CHANCE

Whether on the road or at home, at the beginning of each series you played against a team, there would be a team meeting. The manager would go over each opposing hitter and how we were going to pitch and play him. The team would position itself, both outfield and infield, according to the way our pitcher was going to pitch to him.

Then the pitcher and catcher would get together to discuss their plans. You also knew the teams you played against did the same thing for your team. Nothing is left to chance in the Major Leagues.

SUPERSTITIONS

Therefore, it may seem funny to learn about all the superstitions baseball players have had. They are notorious for their superstitions and quirky methods of preparing to play or keep streaks alive. Players may adopt certain routines or be attached to certain items. The more odd the superstition, the more memorable it is. And as bizarre as they may seem to everyone else, they are dire necessities to those players who hold to them.

To name a couple, I have seen players refuse to shave until they get a hit. On the other hand, I have seen players refuse to shave while they are in a hitting streak. The list goes on: Players believe in wearing the same undergarments, playing catch with the same person before each game, eating the same food each game day, sitting in the same place in the dugout, placing

An Inside-the-Park Look

their cap and glove in the same place, using the same shower stall and using the same kind of soap.

The most popular superstition surrounds one's bat. Even in the Minor League, everyone has his own bat. However, in the Major League, your bat is personalized with your signature engraved on it. Everyone signed with a bat company, which was at that time either Louisville Slugger or Adirandack. We had one bat for batting practice and our precious game bat. You let no one touch your game bat. You regretted it when your favorite game bat was broken or cracked.

Other idiosyncrasies were even stranger: drawing a line on deck or in the batter's box and making sure to step around it but never cross it, and spitting over the same shoulder or in the same spot.

I never believed those things attributed to your success or failure. There are so many things you have to think about in baseball that adding to them did not make sense to me. When all is said and done, nobody cared about how you did or what you did to prepare. What really mattered was getting the job done, day in and day out. When you don't, you're outta there, as the umpire says. It's no secret that only those who help the team to win consistently, whether on offense or defense, can stay.

By the way, I have to admit that every time I went to bat, I would smooth the dirt out in the batter's box. Some may call that a superstition, but I called it a preference. Other batters would make holes in the dirt, and I just felt so much better when the surface was smooth.

Chapter Eleven

Baseball in Black and White

In my day, although segregation was in full force, black and white baseball players seemed to get along fine. A player was a player, and a person was a person. Color was not a problem in my career.

There was, however, an unwritten law that you could only have so many black players on your team. Therefore, we had to compete against each other for position. However, it didn't seem to be true for the Dodgers and the Pirates; they had far more black players than other teams.

Black players had a special bond with one another. They used to get together whenever the chance presented itself. All through the Minor Leagues, the black players would get together and share places to eat and play the game repeatedly. It was so nice to go to a city you didn't know and be led around–even driven–by your opponent. We shared information about how we were treated by our team and our organization. We took care of each other by reminding each other to be careful where you go and how you act. After all, we stood out as though we had on a Batman suit and cape. We played hard against one another, no doubt about that, yet we were like brothers off the field.

My Time at Bat — A Story of Perseverance

For those of us who made it to the big league, that didn't change. We were even more protective because we knew we were always under the microscope. We would hang out with one another and do our best to make it easy or as good as we could in our hometown.

I am so thrilled to tell you that during spring training, it was a daily occurrence to sit and discuss what was going on with your team, the city, other teams and places to eat–not to mention where to go to buy clothes or anything else. We gave one another advice about being Major League players. The players offered a lot of do's and don'ts. It was practice for when the season began and black players made it their business to get together. It is safe to say we took care of one another, reminding one another that it was getting late and offering rides to one another's hotel. It was no big thing to hang out after the game, mainly giving players rides to eat or to one of the favorite places to go have a beer. When we went to eat or have a beer at a black-owned establishment, you seldom, if ever, had to sign autographs because black people didn't worry you, and they knew who you were, and it was common that they kept their distance.

Black people were aware of what went on. For example, when we would go somewhere, someone would say, "Nice game," or, "That was a great catch," or even, "That home run was great." It was a way of life. The black players were in their element. They could relax, and that was a relief. It was nice to be able to leave the game at the stadium, to go to a place where you could be yourself. I spent all of my 11 years in the American League, so I don't know where the hangout places were in the National League, but we all got together whenever possible.

I remember the time Dodgers shortstop Murray Wills called me to get information on Whitey Ford, as the Dodgers and Yankees were about to play each other in the World Series. I gave him a rundown on what to look for.

Blacks also bonded in the premier black magazine, *Ebony*—which used to feature all of the black players to let people know who was where during the 1960s and 1970s.

While blacks bonded with one another, blacks and whites also got along well on all the teams I was on. After all, we share the same dream in the Minor Leagues: making the big league. In the big league, each teammate is glad for one another because winning the game is your main objective.

Baseball in Black and White

Some black and white people were best friends. There are some things that happened in baseball, just as in any other job relation between blacks and whites, but none that stood out on my teams. It's a funny thing, the more you talk to one another, as we did all the time, the more you realized that there are few differences. I know each person respected the others for what they could do and would go all out for his teammate, against any opposition. In other words, the rules were the same, regardless of your race or origin.

I've been asked many times how I got along with my white teammates, the answer, pure and simple, is just fine. I loved them. When in the clubhouse, on the field, in an airplane or on the team bus, you may not talk to certain teammates because you are engaged in conversation with someone else or because you may not be close to them—not because of race. I often found that with white teammates, there was little difference in where we came from and what it took to get where we were. Our likes and dislikes were very much the same; they wanted for their family as much comfort as I wanted for mine. In the course of a season, you engage in discussion on all types of issues like anybody would. People are people. They come together as special talented players, but they are human beings with the same common goals.

In any walk of life, I've found that what you give is what you get back, regardless of color. It's as clear as black and white. Prove yourself to be true, show a smile first, speak down to no one, go out of your way to help others, don't give excuses and be willing to do what you can. Then you can expect a little help from your fellow man.

Chapter Twelve

Life After Baseball

I had a rewarding baseball career. I will always look back on it with fond memories. In fact, I still have some of my game balls—ones autographed by my teammates. Among those in my collection: the ball from my one and only grand slam. I also have the balls from my 999th and 1,000th hits, both of which were home runs. Playing professional baseball was a dream come true. I never saw myself doing anything else. I know it doesn't sound human, but all you think about is being ready, season by season, game by game. However, it came time for my baseball career to end.

THE DREADED PINK SLIP

I opened my mail one day in January to find a "pink slip." That meant the organization opted not to renew my contract. I can't really say I was surprised. Honestly, I was somewhat relieved because I was not getting the amount of play I was used to. I was thirty-seven years old and hadn't stolen a base the last two seasons. My legs had been one of my biggest weapons. And any athlete will tell you he won't last forever.

MY TIME AT BAT — A STORY OF PERSEVERANCE

Unlike most players, I didn't worry about what I would do after my baseball career ended. That's funny because nobody quietly retires from baseball; after all, you think you can still play at any age. I had had a rewarding career and was embarking upon a new one that was tailor-made for me.

During the off season of 1963, I had joined The Roving Leaders within the D.C. Department of Recreation. I continued with the department during future off seasons. When I received my release from Cleveland in winter 1971, I joined The Roving Leaders full time. In addition, in January 1972, it just so happened that Howard University was looking for a baseball coach. I interviewed for the position. I was hired part time as head baseball coach one week later.

Instead of focusing on myself, I worked hard at getting Howard ready for the season. My Major League knowledge was invaluable. So I didn't really miss spring training. I was in spring training for my players.

Teaching them was a given. Because I had played nearly every position in the Major Leagues, I was more than qualified to coach them. Because I was always a catcher at heart, training the pitchers was second nature.

It wasn't easy for the recreation department to have me as a full-time employee because my coaching job was also time-consuming. I am very much indebted to both the department and the university for their flexibility. They were a most important part of my life.

So you can see, for me, there was life after Major League Baseball. How sweet it is to come out of the big league into college baseball and coach youngsters. It was my pleasure to inspire them to become excellent in their chosen field. After all, in college, students are trying to find their place in day-to-day living.

My life after Major League Baseball continued to be truly enjoyable. Although I was paid for my jobs, I really loved the role I played in the lives of those youngsters. They were my main concern, daily. People are good and bad. Some are also very different or even difficult. However, if you give of yourself or act on your best behavior, things will work in your favor. Experience is the best teacher. Since I had been exposed to so much, I had a lot to give, share and teach. But no matter what, if you always give respect, usually you will get it in return.

Life After Baseball

CATCHING ON TO COACHING

We practiced twice a day to get things done. I had to be careful because unlike in the pros, not all players were good. In fact, some of them were downright pitiful. I had to learn not to expect too much from every player. However, my team turned out to be good enough to win the Mid Eastern Athletic Conference championship my first year coaching. It was the first baseball championship Howard had ever won.

We won again in 1973, 1975 and 1976. From 1976 until 1984, baseball was discontinued as an MEAC championship. Once MEAC put baseball back into championship play, we won again in 1984, 1986 and 1998. No other MEAC team has won more championships or more games—we won more than 600 games. I am now in Howard University's Hall of Fame.

Until I came to Howard, the team had played only within the MEAC or against other black schools. I vowed to change that and made sure we played against all the local colleges. We even traveled to other parts of the country to play. I wanted the players to have a well-rounded group of opponents. Sometimes we won; sometimes we lost. But at least we got to play.

I had plenty of players who signed pro, but only two—Jerry Davis and Milt Thompson—have made it to the big league. In fact, both played in the World Series. I was proud that they were afforded the opportunity I never had.

Although not everyone made a career in baseball, I am proud of them all. It is so great to have had so many young men graduate from college and go on to work in many fields. I couldn't begin to name them all, but when I see them every now and then, my heart is glad and proud. So many of them call me Dad. I believe it's because I tried to teach them about more than

With Howard University. 1998

MY TIME AT BAT — A STORY OF PERSEVERANCE

baseball–that a man should work, take care of his family, help others, be conscientious, and accept and trust the Lord Jesus Christ and allow Him to lead you in all your ways.

Overall, coaching really was a full-time job, but you do what you have to do. If I taught my players anything, I taught them to be on time. Many a player has been left in D.C. when the bus would leave for road trips; some players even have missed the bus home. I remember when the bus was pulling off from the athletic dorm on our way to Florida and the driver spotted a tardy player running to catch the bus, luggage in tow. The driver asked me, "Do you want me to stop?" I retorted, "We're not in Florida yet, are we?" There was no "CP Time" in my program. My motto was, "I didn't leave you; you left yourself."

TOGETHER AGAIN

For twenty years, Checo was my assistant coach at Howard. He did the non-paying job with pride. In twenty-eight years, I was only thrown out of one Howard game. Checo was thrown out of at least two games each year. He would yell, "Do you think you are in South Africa?" to the umpires down South. "Shake your head, your eyes are stuck," was another favorite line of his. He led the NCAA in being tossed, no doubt. But I am grateful

Checo and I playing golf in Arizona. We took the Howard team to Arizona to play Arizona State University. 1999

Life After Baseball

for his years of service. I could never repay God for the love we have for each other.

We haven't let the fact that he is a diehard Dallas Cowboys fan come between us because at my house, it's "Hail to the Redskins." Don't even get him started talking about the Cowboys vs. anybody. He considers himself "The Cowboys' Twelfth Man." In spite of that, I thank God that he's my brother and that we are so close. We are fortunate to have each other. Our brother Patches passed away some ten years ago. We all miss him. We called him "The Ambassador of I-95," for he would get on that highway in a heartbeat, sharing his special blend of sunshine and joy.

REACHING OUT

When I wasn't coaching, I was placed in certain areas of the city to deal with hard-to-reach youth as a roving leader. My task was to be there for them—whether it was at home, school or court—and show them I cared. You can't fool kids. If your actions don't reflect your words, they will feel you can't be trusted. At-risk kids usually only respect people they trust and can depend on. Unfortunately, in many cases, there are few people they can depend on.

The young people I worked with thank me, even now, for taking them places and getting them involved in activities they never would have experienced otherwise. I not only gave my time, but also spent my own money when I had to. Thanksgiving and Christmas are special days for most people, but for some, they are depressing. I made sure certain families had a turkey and other things to make their holiday season a happy one. I learned that when you give people things they need, it restores their belief in people.

The last twelve years, I had been stationed on playgrounds. I was responsible for showing kids new games and teaching them to be productive members of society. I would tell them that they could do whatever they set their minds to, that they could see their dreams realized if they worked at it now.

We used sports and games to drive home the principles of bettering their skills and being the best they could be. We always had something special for holidays and special times such as Halloween, Recreation Day and the Martin Luther King Jr. holiday. I introduced as many kids as I could to golf, and I am pleased that I did.

MY TIME AT BAT — A STORY OF PERSEVERANCE

For some of the kids I worked with, survival was an issue. The playground or recreation centers were places where they could come and be treated as human beings. Some of them had to come for food, money, advice, safety, clothing, peace of mind and, of course, recreation. There they could simply be kids. As smart as I thought I was and as many experiences as I had had, those kids at the recreation department taught me a thing or two. I learned to be a good listener. After all, another person's point of view is as important as yours. I'm far from perfect, but I find it easy not to hurt a person's feelings because I treat people as I want to be treated.

SPEAKING OF GOLF

The game of golf became a major part of my post-Major League lifestyle. I enjoy playing in charitable golf tournaments across the country. One tournament I remember well is the 1982 NFL Alumni Redskins Chapter Tournament, held at Indian Spring Country Club. I was the celebrity substitute for Mark Mosley, a former place kicker for the Redskins, and assigned to a team of four other guys from Fairfax, Virginia: John Gilmore, Bob Batal, Mal Bennett and Scotty Buzzwell. Thirty-three fivesomes—165 golfers—played in the event on the chief course. Former Redskin Roy Jefferson's team came in second. Coach Joe Gibbs, Joe Theisman, Brig Owens, Chris Hamburger, Ray Nitsche, Jim Taylor, Andy Styncula, Bill Dudley and Bobby Mitchell—all former Redskins—played in the tournament as well.

We shot an amazing sixteen under par to run away with the tournament. We won an all-expenses-paid trip to Hilton Head, South Carolina, to play against the winners of the other NFL team tournaments. This was called the NFL Alumni Golf Super Bowl. The tournament was held at Harbor Town Golf

NFL Alumni Redskins Chapter Tournament, Indian Springs Country Club, Silver Spring, MD. 1982

Life After Baseball

Course, where the PGA plays each year. This time, we shot fifteen under par to win the tournament. The highlight was a double eagle on hole fifteen.

We were awarded Super Bowl rings and NFL golf bags. That ring was something to behold: eighteen-karat gold set in emerald with a solid gold golf ball in the center. We were also honored at a welcome-home luncheon. We went back next year the defending champions, but the tournament was shortened due to rain, and we lost. Since that time, I've been barred from the tournament, as the football players were embarrassed that I was a baseball player.

THE ALUMNI ASSOCIATION IS BORN

When I returned from the NFL Alumni Golf Super Bowl, the Alexandria Dukes Minor League team was having a promotional game. Former Senators Fred Valentine, Jim Hannah and I were invited. I asked Jim if there was a baseball alumni association. He said he would call around to check and get back with me. I mentioned that I had won the NFL Alumni Golf Super Bowl and would like to start one for baseball, if one didn't exist.

We found out there was no alumni association for baseball. So we began to meet on a monthly basis to start one. We gathered all the baseball alumni we could from the metropolitan area and Baltimore to rally support. The baseball commissioner, Bowie Knune, invited us to New York to present our proposal. Jim Hannah, Brooks Robinson, Fred Valentine and I made the trip to see the commissioner and American and National League presidents. They loved our proposal, and the league presidents gave us $30,000 to start the association. The Major League Baseball Players' Alumni Association was formed in 1982.

We wrote bylaws and retained a lawyer, Sam Moore, to guide us through the legal processes. Sam was a key player who advised us of what we could and could not do; he made sure everything was above board. After we received our nonprofit status, we decided to hire John Horshack to set up an office in Virginia and run the association, as we all had full-time jobs.

Later, the headquarters was moved to Colorado Springs, Colorado. Membership in the MLBPAA has climbed to more than 4,800, of which, approximately 2,800 are former Major League players and 1,000 current players are also Alumni members. The remainder of membership is com-

MY TIME AT BAT — A STORY OF PERSEVERANCE

VALUE STATEMENT

MAJOR LEAGUE BASEBALL ®
PLAYERS ALUMNI

We believe that:
The traditions of baseball reflect values in society that are the best of American life

Our association is dedicated to protect the dignity of the game through former major league players

We achieve our beliefs by:
Demonstrating through our leadership our commitment to American values

Promoting a passion for the game of baseball as the best for American life, its values, heritage and heroes

Serving the unique needs of the players

prised of Minor League players, umpires, managers, coaches, front office personnel, media and fans.

At this writing, we are celebrating our 20th Anniversary. The MLBPAA provides players with the proper vehicle to become involved in charitable causes nationwide. We conduct baseball clinics and golf outings around the country. We are currently holding forty to fifty golf tournaments per year nationwide and have raised more than $5 million for local charities.

Our charge is to promote the game of baseball, involve former Major League players in community activities, inspire today's youth through positive sports images and raise funds to support important charitable causes. Alumni members understand that as one of only a few living Major League players, they belong to a select group that has the unique ability to advance and encourage the sport of baseball and the values associated with the game. The MLBPAA is an organization where a player's drive for excellence and achievement on the field could continue long after he took his last steps off the diamond. Many of the game's leading players have gravitated to the Alumni Association. Alumni members include Hall of Famers, All-Stars, Cy Young Award winners and Gold Glove Award recipients.

I am proud that the association was my idea. I am still quite active and serve as a vice president. Fred and Jim both serve on the board of directors. The president is Brooks Robinson. The MLBPAA also owns two subsidiaries that include Major League Alumni Marketing (MLAM) and Major League Alumni Services (MLAS). Former Major Leaguers find the Alumni Association to be a vital, constructive instrument in giving back to the game of baseball.

Life After Baseball

L to R-Jim Hannah, Ferguson Jenkins, Bert Campanaris, and myself at a MLBPAA Golf Tournament in Washington, D.C. 2000

I mentioned earlier that I visit Cleveland each year. That is because the alumni association puts on a clinic at Jacobs Field there. It is a beautiful facility. We all have lunch with the Waw Whoo Club and hold a golf tournament. It is so much fun to see former teammates and fans during the three-day event. I look forward to it each year.

A NEW CHAPTER IN LIFE

After thirty-one years with the Department of Recreation and twenty-eight years at Howard, I decided my time was up. So in 1999, I retired from both. It is quite a joy to be able to go to the golf course when I please. I hope most of you will experience it some day. God is good, and He promised long life to those who honor their parents (Exodus 12:12).

For twenty-eight years, I had to play golf early in the morning. I would get in nine holes and then have to go off to work. Now I play nine, eighteen, even thirty-six holes. I don't have to rush off to work anymore. A bunch of golfers and I travel to a different golf course each Thursday. Sometimes we have as many as twenty golfers, but usually it's twelve.

MY TIME AT BAT — A STORY OF PERSEVERANCE

Golf is a game you can really enjoy playing. It's great not to have any real aches or pains that would keep you from playing. You get to enjoy some of the best courses. Furthermore, while you are on the golf course, the world does not exist because it takes all your concentration to play a good game–even though the ball does not move and the other players give you all the respect in the world by being quiet when you are about to make a shot.

Even though it is so enjoyable, golf is by far the toughest sport to play, become good at and remain good at. Even if you practice a lot, you will find a part of your game will be missing.

In no other sport do you have no opponent but the course itself. To hit the ball exactly where you want to is difficult. In fact, just to hit it in the direction you want it to go in is tough. Most people think golf is so easy. Well, I've got news for them. Try it. It's so nice to have a good round, but sometimes you have a round where you might not have had but a few pars. It is hard to believe, but it happens. I enjoy being able to play, whether I'm having a good or bad round.

I am so happy and grateful that I am able to enjoy not only the game of golf, but also my surroundings. On most golf courses, the cut of the course with trees, flowers, water and sand is beautiful. I know God has been very good to me. Whether on the golf course or not, being thankful is a way of life that I enjoy.

Not everyone is able to play golf, but people should find something to do with their time that they find most enjoyable. When it comes to athletics, one has to be truthful, for everyone would like to be a pro, but the odds are so stacked against it. This may sound a little off beat, but you could be one of the best players and not get a chance at the pros. Nothing is wrong with being a star in high school and getting a scholarship to college that would put you in position to get a diploma and become a leader in whatever field you might choose.

It just so happened that the hobby I chose turned into a career, and enabled me to go all over the country playing alumni golf tournaments for charity and spending time with ex-Major League players. What a life. I really wish each working person could retire and live as I do. My advice would be to start on a hobby soon that will make you happy. That is the bottom line–happiness.

Life After Baseball

My church also has been a source of great happiness in my life. Integrity Church International is a non-denominational, full-gospel, independent church. We speak in tongues and lift holy hands to our God. I am the leader of a group that meets every Wednesday morning from ten until noon. We call it Care Group. We praise and worship our Lord Jesus and study from the printed lessons approved by our pastors, Apostle Jim and Jean Thompson.

I am also a leader in the prison ministry. For eleven years now, I have gone to Lorton to fellowship with the inmates. Let me tell you, when I let God lead me in the service, the inmates and I just enjoy the ride the Holy Spirit takes us on. It is sheer enjoyment. I just love being used by God.

OUR FLOWER FOREVER BLOOMS

In life, just as there are mountaintops you reach, there are valleys you must walk through. One of our battles as a family was with Jonquil's health. She fought valiantly, but in the end, her heart stopped.

What a home going she had, for to be absent from the body is to be present with the Lord. So in early 2002, she went on to be with Him. She doesn't have to struggle or suffer any longer. And that gives me a sense of relief.

Daddies like to think their daughters love them a little more than they love anyone else. No doubt, Joni made not just me, but everyone feel special. She was a giver, and most of the time, it was her love she gave. God blessed Joni with so much love, and she had no problem sharing it. She had a smile that was a joy to see. She was so pleasant to be around. She gave us plenty of joy. I gave all my children everything I could. After all, you live for your kids. I will always remember the times we had. But more than that, I won't forget what a great person she was. She was a loving daughter, wife and mother.

Our flower will forever be with us. "You fought a good fight. You kept the faith. Well done you good and faithful servant."

MY TIME AT BAT — A STORY OF PERSEVERANCE

jon·quil [j'ngkwl] *noun*: flowering plant of the amaryllis family. Its small, graceful flowers grow several to a stalk. It has intensely fragrant, golden-yellow, short-tubed flowers, is widely cultivated as an ornamental, and is also used in perfumery. Jonquils represent happy renewal and promise and are one of the first harbingers of spring.

Our Beloved Joni...

"Joni, you weren't just my wife; you were my best friend." –John

"A giver of love with your beautiful smile shall I remember all of my days." –Daddy

"Miss Joni, you were my flower. You will always remain a flower in my life, my heart and my memories." –Mommy

"You were the sunshine of my life." –Chucky

"My bright star has faded...a profound loss to my life. However, I smile because I *know* you are dancing all over those streets of gold." –Kim

"The life of the party, the joy of the day, your infectious smile and formidable strength were precious, rare and sweet." –Tiffany

"Mommy, every game I play, I'll look up for you." –Eric

"You'll forever be in my heart." –John John

"When I say my prayers at night, I'll think of you." –Terria

"I've never seen you angry; every time I saw you, you were smiling." –Grandma

"You were walking joy." –Derwin

Chapter Thirteen

Baseball Today

Major League Baseball has changed quite a bit over the last thirty years, since I was sporting a uniform. While I don't think the players are better today than in my day, I do think that because of the way things have changed, the players are in better condition, are stronger and, in most cases, are larger. For example, when I played, you could not find a batting cage in your stadium. Now stadiums have batting cages and weight rooms. That's out of sight. That means a player can work out daily and hit year-round. We didn't do that because the opportunity and equipment was not there.

Speaking of equipment, that's better also—the balls, bats, gloves and shoes. But no, the players are not better, in my opinion, because the game has not changed that much. One can only throw but so fast. One can only run so fast, field balls so good, hit a ball so far. You are where you are because you are one of the best in the world—just as the best in the world were in the big league thirty years ago.

Another thing that has changed, of course, is players' pay. Players today are not overpaid, in my opinion, but the cost of living has increased dramatically since 1961-1971. People with any job are making a lot more money today. And remember, professional athletes are skilled and talented people.

My Time at Bat — A Story of Perseverance

CEOs and entertainers get top dollar because of their production. Why shouldn't a player who produces get paid for what he does? Fans are still packing the stadiums to see the very best players.

2001: WHAT A SEASON

And the very best players is definitely what baseball fans saw in 2001. Fans were treated in a rare season. Barry Bonds' seventy-three home runs is unreal. How about all those walks and a record slugging percentage? And his fourth-time MVP award. What a special player Barry Bonds is. How about Seattle and its record-setting games won? Iechiro Suzuki was named Rookie of the Year *and* MVP, with a batting average of .350, more than fifty stolen bases and more than 240 hits. What a season he had.

Randy Johnson was in a zone–along with his Diamondback teammate Chuck Shilling. Sammy Sousa had his fourth straight year of fifty or more home runs. Roger Clemmons won his fourth Cy Young Award. What a year Alex Rodriguez ("A. Rod") had hitting over .300, with more than 150 RBIs and more than fifty home runs. Seattle had a fantastic season. There were many other players who had great seasons.

What a season. What a playoff. We then were treated to the most exciting World Series ever, with Arizona coming back in the ninth inning to beat

L to R–Myself, Bobby Tolan, Kevin Bass and Jimmy Wynn at an alumni affair in Washington, D.C. 2000

Baseball Today

the Yankees, who had won three straight World Series. 2001 was a super season for our super sport. I can hardly wait for the next season to begin. Congratulations. The game will miss Mark McGuire, Cal Ripken and Tony Gwynn. They were good for the game. I am proud to be part of the chosen few who make baseball the great game that it is.

A LIFETIME OF BASEBALL

Today, I can enjoy as much baseball as I would like. Once you have been in the Major Leagues for nine years, the baseball commissioner's office sends you a lifetime pass. It's a beautiful gold plate, about the size of a credit card with your name engraved on it. The pass comes in a nice leather wallet and will permit you and one guest to attend regular-season games in both leagues. What a prized possession. Every time I use mine, the people at the gates don't seem to know about the pass, but they are kind and say, "I remember you." I don't get to use it much because when you have spent all your life in parks and stadiums playing and watching baseball at all levels, you don't have a strong desire to attend baseball games.

Furthermore, since I live in Washington, D.C., I have to drive over to Baltimore, which is 45 miles each way, to see a game. To avoid rush-hour traffic, I have to leave early to see batting practice and more or less spend a day at the ball yard. By the seventh inning, I'm ready to leave to beat the traffic out of the parking lot. No matter who the Orioles are playing, the parking lots are full because every game is a sellout. Camden Yards is a great place to watch the game. Very little was spared when it was built. I catch the last inning on the car radio. For these reasons, I would like to see baseball back in Washington, D.C.

I have used my pass only a few times. The lifetime pass is no good for the All Star Game, playoffs or World Series. I have found that it allows you entrance into the stadium for those special games, but after that, you are on your own. That is no way to treat us former players. I wish that would change. I don't see why a seat or seats at a special event are not put aside for us. They should set aside a place for a certain number of ex-players. How can you allow an ex-player and his guest to enter a stadium but leave them to standing room only? It is an insult.

MY TIME AT BAT — A STORY OF PERSEVERANCE

BASEBALL IN D.C.

The fact that there is no team in Washington, D.C., our nation's capital, is a shame. So many things have changed since thirty years ago, when we last had a team there, we are well able to support and delight in our team. I am sure the people here would like nothing better than to have a baseball team that they could call their own.

There is no doubt that the city would support its team, for there is a hunger for baseball. For seventy-five years, Washington was a good supporter of a losing team. Now with free agents, you have to have money. We have many people in place who have money and want to be part of making baseball a thing of the future. I can tell you that there is still a Washington Senators fan club, and we also have *Nat's News*, which keeps up on former players. Our mayor and City Council are in full support of a baseball team. I think it's going to happen in the near future. If baseball were to come to D.C., I would certainly spend a few nights and days at the yard again, rooting for our team.

> *Baseball commissioner Bud Selig said that he thinks a team might move and that Washington is the "prime candidate" for a relocated team. Selig is in Phoenix, Arizona, at a meeting of team owners. The original plan was to eliminate two failing baseball teams: most likely the Montreal Expos and the Minnesota Twins. But that plan has been blocked by a court in Minnesota. That leaves moving a team from a city that has poor attendance to one where more people might attend the games.*
> –Washington Post C10, January 18, 2002

> ***March 31, 2003: Day of deliverance?*** *For the first time, the highest-ranking official in Major League Baseball has confirmed that Washington stands a good chance to get a team, probably in 2003. This is huge... Thanks for your support, Bud Selig, and don't let us down this time. We'll see you at RFK Stadium on Monday, March 31, 2003, when the brand-new Washington Nationals—no other name should even be considered—open the National League season after President Bush unlimbers his pitching arm. Let's play ball. Please.*
> –Dick Heller, Washington Times C5, January 19, 2002

Baseball Today

Washington Historical Baseball Society Presents Nats Fest 2000. Top L to R–Jim Lemon, myself, Don Lock, Tom Cheney, Bennie Daniels. Bottom L to R–Lou Sleater, Barry Shetrone, Pedro Ramas, J.W. Porter

Many things have happened in baseball, and I would like nothing better than to see the best players in the world here. There is something special about great baseball peanuts, hot dogs and beer–what a way to spend a day. The fans in Washington are eager to see their team. Everyone in the leagues seems to be hitting home runs. We, too, want to root and see our own team go deep.

I rate the fans in Washington as some of the best baseball has to offer. They really stuck with the team in my day, although we lost more than a hundred games a season and finished last three years, escaping the cellar in 1964. We never thought we would lose that much. We told one another that we would get them the next day. I know I did give my all every day.

Take my word for it: Washington is a Major League city that deserves a team of its own. Just think, after all this time without a team, with interleague play, people would get to see players in both leagues. The people who can make it happen need to know that our city is really hot for a team. So many things are in place; we have done a lot to ready ourselves for it. I just wish it would be soon because great fans have been on hold much too long.

MY TIME AT BAT — A STORY OF PERSEVERANCE

I was so honored to be inducted into the Washington Hall of Stars in 1984. This article appeared in the Howard University *Capstone*, October 22, 1984

It was only fitting. After more than 20 years of playing major league baseball and coaching the sport at Howard, Chuck Hinton was being recognized for his service in both.

On Oct. 14, the former Washington Senators star was inducted into the illustrious Washington Hall of Stars at halftime of the Washington Redskins-Dallas Cowboys football game at Robert F. Kennedy Stadium.

The Washington Hall of Stars recognizes local sports professionals and executives who have made outstanding contributions in the Washington area. Hinton was inducted along with two former Redskins, Vince Promuto and Len Hauss, Washington Bullets General Manager Bob Ferry and Deane Beman, commissioner of the Professional Golfers Association.

"This is a great thrill for me," said Hinton. "I credit God for giving me talent, and myself for the endurance. I enjoyed my years playing professional baseball, moreover, I enjoy working with the young people."

In the university's 94-year baseball history, there has never been a coach as successful as Hinton. Winning has been his trademark.

Prior to his arrival in 1972, only three teams in the last nine seasons had finished above the .500 mark. Hinton's first two squads posted 13-9 and 14-5 records; over the next three years, the Bison reeled off consecutive 20-plus victory campaigns.

Howard also captured three Mid-Eastern Athletic Conference baseball crowns during his first four seasons.

In his 12 years of coaching at Howard, Hinton compiled a 301-293 mark and has had 18 players drafted into the major leagues with two currently playing—Jerry Davis of the San Diego Padres and Milton Thompson of the Atlanta Braves.

When conference play was terminated in 1976, Hinton, undaunted, continued Bison competition as an independent, and concluded the season with a 21-16 mark. In 1984, the MEAC reinstituted baseball and Howard picked up where it left off with the conference title. At the conference tournament at South Carolina State in Orangeburg, Howard won the round-robin competition with a 4-1 record. Hinton was named the outstanding coach, and center-

cont'd, other side

Chuck Hinton poses with his personal portrait presented by the executive board of the Washington Hall of Stars during the pre-induction luncheon at the D.C. Armory.

fielder Rozier Jordan was selected the most valuable player.

"He is a great coach to play for," said Glenn Harris, a former all-conference performer during the 1974 season. "Coach Hinton coached with a major league perspective. His favorite saying was 'keep the ball between the lines.' He made me a better ball player and more aware of the game. It was a pleasure to play for him," said Harris, who is now sports director at the university's WHUR-FM radio station.

As a player, Hinton was outstanding. The Rocky Mount, N.C., native groomed his talents at Booker T. Washington High School, and later at Shaw University in Raleigh, N.C. He broke into the major league with the Washington Senators in 1961 and became the only .300 hitter in the franchise's history. Hinton played every major position except pitcher.

During his 10 professional seasons, Hinton also played with the Cleveland Indians and the California Angels. One of the highlights of his career was an appearance in the 1967 All-Star game.

"I have always loved the sport of baseball," said Hinton. "It has been very good to me. Coaching also has been an enjoyable experience. I like to think that I am contributing to the student-athlete's character and helping him to become more of a well-rounded individual."

Inducted into the Washington Hall of Stars Oct. 14 at RFK Stadium were Chuck Hinton, Vince Promuto, Bob Ferry, Len Hauss and Deane Beman.

Chapter Fourteen

For Love of the Game

Whether in D.C. or any other city, real fans love the game of baseball as much as many of the players do. And being naturally talented in the sport and part of a chosen few in the Major Leagues, the players love their career opportunity. But don't believe for a second that it all comes easy. It takes a great deal of hard work, preparation and mental strength to perform and contribute to a win for your team on a daily basis.

THE REAL FAN

I have been a fan of baseball since I was a child. As a fan, you learn early on to keep the game score card and, of course, keep record of the game. You know the starting lineup.

Baseball might be the only sport for which fans keep records of the games. I also think baseball might be the only sport that would allow you to record things you see because you have the time. When there is a double play around the horn, you simply put 5-4-3, which means the third baseman, to the second baseman to the first baseman. The real fan knows that every position has a number, starting with the pitcher (1), then the catcher (2), first baseman (3), second baseman (4), third baseman (5), shortstop (6), left fielder (7), center fielder (8) and right fielder (9). You might have a little problem in a run-down put out, which could go 1 to 3 to 6 to 4 to 2.

Many people say baseball is too slow. Well, you will not hear that from a true fan because he knows that the battle between the pitcher and batter is where the game is really played. He knows the planning that has gone on before the game. He knows there is a lot of strategy and excitement some fans may not see. The pitcher is trying his best to get the batter to hit his pitch that he plans to get him with. Then the batter is waiting for the pitch that he knows he can really drive. You may be privileged to see a no-hitter or, better yet, a perfect game. Or maybe you'll see a one- or two-run game. In baseball, you never know what you will get. When you think you are going to get a one- or two-run game, you just might get a slugfest.

Still, a real fan knows this and has fun no matter what. Keep your record of the game; after all, you just might record something special. Then you can go back in the records that show you were there when it happened, even five, ten, fifteen or thirty years earlier. A real fan knows a lot about the game and expects to see it played at its best. I am sure you get a special thrill when you see a young player improve somewhat every year. What one wants to do is be a great fan each year, just like the players work so hard to be great. A real fan appreciates a great play or hit, even when it's from the other team. After all, we should like what's right and be the first to down what's wrong. There is no place in baseball for a fan to call a player names or for a player to yell an obscenity to a fan.

WHEN YOU GOT IT, YOU GOT IT

The real athletes, those who excel, are born with their talent. In my opinion, talent comes from the womb. I don't care how much you practice or lift weights, it won't make you throw harder. You are born with a great arm, or you are not. You can take all the batting practice in this world; it's no guarantee you will hit good pitching. You can run every day, three times a day, but you have great speed, or you don't. Then there is that fine line of players who cannot deliver in the clutch (game-winning situation).

For Love of the Game

The Reunion Game. The 1966 Washington Senators vs. The 1966 Baltimore Orioles. The Senators won 3 – 2. I drove in the winning RBI. That was a lot of fun. Also pictured, Don Lock. Photo courtesy of Lawrence Johnson. 1986

MY TIME AT BAT — A STORY OF PERSEVERANCE

You can take ground balls every day, sometimes twice a day or more, and you won't have soft or quick hands. The same can be said about fly balls. You may practice for many hours yet may never be able to see the ball come off the bat, turn your back to it and run exactly where it's coming down to make the catch. You also are born with a gift for hitting. Running bases or even stealing bases is a gift that you are born with as well.

There is no doubt that you can work on all of those skills and become better, but never a great player at the Major League level. Why do you think baseball teams have scouts all around the world looking for those skills that will lead to becoming a pro? It's a shame that if you don't run a certain speed or throw with eye-opening speed or hit with great power, you don't get a chance at pro ball. You have to test well, process certain skills, hit with power, field grounders and fly balls well, have a good arm and run fast.

It's seldom that a player gets signed without having two out of three of those skills. The superstar can do it all, plus hit home runs or pitch great. Of course, there are always exceptions. A pitcher might not be able to throw strikes with more than one pitch, but maybe he can throw ninety-five miles per hour-plus and is known as big-league cheese, the blue darter, the dark one, the hummer, lightning, smoke and many other terms all meaning very fast.

Many of you may never get to face a pitcher who throws ninety-five-plus. Well, let me tell you, the sound from the catcher's mitt can be frightening. Clap your hands or blink your eyes. That's how fast the ball gets to the plate or into the catcher's mitt after it leaves the pitcher's hand. One might ask, "How did you hit it?" Well, much of the time, you don't. As a big-league hitter, you face pitchers every day who can get it up to that speed, and by doing so, you get used to it and react. The Minor Leagues are also training grounds for getting used to all kinds of pitchers. However, a person who doesn't face it on a regular basis has a hard time seeing the ball, never mind hitting it. But if you are to stay there, you have to deliver more times than not.

USING YOUR HEAD

Besides having the necessary skills, a player needs to have a sharp, quick mind to be successful. One instance where this is necessary is when you need to communicate with baseball signs. While you are at bat or running the bases, you get a sign telling you what the coach wants you to do. For exam-

For Love of the Game

ple, the coach might want a bunt to advance the runner to second base. The coach gives a sign to the hitter and the runner at the same time. Both players must see the sign immediately, then both must also know what to do to make it happen.

The runner must know to see the ball bunted on the ground. He also must not get picked off. He must get a proper lead, see the pitcher deliver the ball to the plate and be ready to go back to first as well as to advance to second base. When all this has been done, he can take off to second base full speed, of course. The hitter must get a strike to bunt and must bunt the ball on the ground. After doing this, his sacrifice job is complete.

Being alert doesn't just mean seeing the signs, but knowing right away what each sign means. There are so many defensive signs, including the infielder, shortstop or second baseman relay, what pitch the pitcher is going to throw, pick-off signs to each base, and the shortstop and second baseman's signs to each other indicating who will be covering the base in case of an attempted stolen base. When a runner is on first base, you see the shortstop and second baseman with their gloves up to their faces as though they are talking to each other. They are signaling each other as to who will be covering the base should the runner take off.

Even outfielders must know the infielder signs for a pick-off. This helps them to be ready to back up the play in case there is an overthrow to keep the runner from advancing an extra base.

Not picking up on the signs can get you into trouble. I truly enjoyed first base because you sort of visit everyone who stops there. You say things such as, "How is everything going?" "Where is a good place to eat?" and "Where do the guys go to have a quiet drink?" You won't believe some of the conversations that go on at first base. However, there are times when a base runner misses a sign because his attention is somewhere else. This is serious business. You are subject to be fined for missing a sign such as hit and run. Why is the hit and run so important? The hitter is supposed to swing at the pitch, trying to hit the ball on the ground because the second baseman has gone to cover the bag because the runner is supposed to be running. It is also important because the manager will try to get a count where the pitcher should try hard to throw a strike.

You must keep your mind focused on all aspects of the game, not just the signs. Chatting with the base runner and not focusing on the next play

My Time at Bat — A Story of Perseverance

sometimes meant I didn't get a jump on a grounder. Then the base runner didn't make an extra base because he was running his mouth.

Each player must think about where he needs to be and what he needs to do in every situation in the field–whether it's backing someone up, covering a base, or being a cut-off man or a relay man. He also needs to think ahead about plays and adjust his positioning if a player hits the ball one way more than the other. This is what the mental part of baseball is about: thinking the play through before it happens. There are times when you have to out-think your opponent.

Baseball is a reaction game. The pitcher throws the ball, the hitter hits it, and the fielders react to it to make a play. Therefore, as a fielder, you have to stay focused every pitch, expecting the ball to be hit to you. Sometimes you see a fielder go through swings between pitches. That is a no-no because your mind is thinking hitting when it should be thinking defense…period. When you put things in the right order, you become a team player. No one really likes a player who openly thinks about himself. When you let your mind wander from defense, that's when the ball is hit your way. Sometimes you make the play, but usually you will misjudge the ball mainly because you were not thinking correctly. That could lead to runs, which could cost the team the game.

It's best to get into the game from the beginning to the end. Sometimes you let your emotions get the best of you, and you really get down on yourself. You soon learn that you are not going to excel all of the time, but you must take things as they are and keep a positive attitude, for there will be another chance for you to do your part, and that is a promise.

When you check the box score, you see almost every game that no errors were committed. That tells you that as a team, the players are good and seldom beat themselves. A good defensive play can win a game also.

On defense, the greatest way to focus is to be ready to field the hardest ball that could be hit to you. When you are ready for that ball, it's easy to adjust to any other hit. On the other hand, not being ready could get you hurt because at all times, the hitter can hit the ball much harder than the pitcher can pitch it. It is not luck when a hitter hits a ball hard. In most cases, the hitter and pitcher both know a day or night ahead of time that they will be facing each other. As a hitter, you know how hard the pitcher

For Love of the Game

throws, what pitches he throws and what pitch he will throw on certain counts or with runners on base. With all this knowledge, the hitter and the pitcher will try to outthink the other. When the pitcher gets the ball where he wants it, he is satisfied with that pitch. However, a hitter may be expecting that pitch at that speed, and many times, a base hit results. That's why it's skill that makes the difference. The same thing holds true for the pitcher. He got you out because he got you to hit the pitch in the location he planned.

When the game is close, you have to be able to keep your mind in the game. It doesn't matter who drives in the winning run or how well the pitchers did their job. The bottom line is the win. You will get your chance to be the hero many times over. Make sure you are ready for the test. Learning to relax is perhaps the main thing you must do. But you can be so relaxed and cool that you look at a third strike. What a shame. Anyone can tell you that if you don't swing, you won't hit the ball. You have to be focused enough that you swing the bat at any ball close to the plate with two strikes against you.

There are times when you do everything just right, yet you hit the ball to someone. During the course of a season, there are many ups and downs like that that you have to be able to handle. There are other times when, even though you know what pitches will help you hit the ball in the desired location, sure enough, you swing at a ball that's way out of the strike zone. You don't mean to do it, but it's one of those things that happens too many times. So you have to be disciplined enough not to swing at bad pitches. Generally, when a pitch is thrown on the inside of the plate, you hit the ball to the left side of the field, if you are a right-handed batter. When it's down the middle of the plate, you hit the ball up the middle. And when it's on the outside of the plate, you drive the ball to the right side of the field.

When at bat, you should focus so much on the pitcher that you don't hear whatever is going on. You have to be able to tune out everything. This is where you make your living. Whatever it takes, keep your mind clear and your body relaxed, ready to do war when you get a pitch to hit. The pitcher is trying his best to get you out. You have to be ready to win the battle each at-bat. Your complete concentration is what you must have—nothing less. Now you are ready for the battle. No one can help you, but you don't need help, for you've got things under control.

MY TIME AT BAT — A STORY OF PERSEVERANCE

I truly can tell you that while at bat, no matter what the situation, I did not hear the fans. I cannot speak for any other player, but to me, everything and everyone was tuned out. All my focus was on the pitcher. After all, you go to bat every ninth time. It is important to give your all because the pitcher you are facing is giving his all to strike you out. If the fans and opposing players distract you, you will have a hard time getting done what you have to accomplish.

LOOKING FOR AN EDGE

Part of the mental aspect of the game is learning to anticipate what the pitcher will throw. As a hitter, you watch a pitcher warm up to see what you can pick up. Every pitcher almost always does the same thing, whatever it may be, before he delivers the ball to home plate. From the wind-up, he may hold the ball in his hand, but while he starts his wind-up, he does the same thing each time he throws a fastball. He even could show something when he brings the ball from his glove before throwing to the plate.

What you are looking for is how he may do it a little differently from other types of pitches.

Then from the stretch position (when runners are on base), a pitcher may do something a little different such as throwing right over the top of his head on a fastball but delivering a curve ball from the top at three-quarters.

You might find it hard to believe, but some pitchers would stick out their tongue when throwing a breaking ball, while some would put a funny frown on their face, and some would grunt. Whatever it is, when it's there for the taking, by all means you use it.

If you watch closely enough, you will find the pitcher's pattern, for it's always there. I've found that pitchers do things by habit, and sometimes they try to change, but most of the time, they go back to doing the same thing. You sometimes keep this habit to yourself. Then again, you might share it with a teammate or two or more. When you know that a certain pitch is being thrown, that is an edge, and you can really put your best swing on it to get good results.

As a base-stealer, you must look at the pitcher to see what he does a little differently. You are looking to pick up on his habits or his first move after

For Love of the Game

the set position—the rules state that a pitcher must come to a complete stop before he delivers the ball. Once you see what his habits are, you know you must go when he does it.

I often am asked who the toughest pitcher was that I ever had to face. My answer is simple: "They all are." That's because there are no easy pitchers in the Major League. If and when you are easy, you will soon be gone.

A CONSTANT LEARNING EXPERIENCE

Once you've hit against a pitcher, it will help you to make every at-bat a learning experience. You have to retain information from your previous times at bat that you will need the next time you face that pitcher. Such information would include what pitch or pitches you hit, what the count was, whether there were runners on base and whether you had a problem picking up the pitcher's release point. The bottom line should be, Did you get a good pitch to hit—one that's in the strike zone and one you can really drive—and did you have a good swing? Whatever you did or didn't do, make sure your next at-bat is a good one.

Hitting is a skill, but you have to do a lot of homework to get the job done. You know who you face. The next day, while you are lying in bed, you go over what the pitcher will throw you in the entire count situation. You know his best pitch; you know how much his curve ball will curve and how much his breaking ball will break.

You go over what stood out about this pitcher. Have you picked up clues as to what pitch is coming? You do this as your homework and part of your duty as a professional. Then when you've gone over and over this, don't go to sleep until you are sure you've done everything that will help you get the pitch you are looking for in that situation.

You do that night after night, keeping in your head things that help you. A team will try to pitch you and play you a certain way. You have to be aware of this. I was a first-ball hitter, meaning I knew the pitcher would be trying to get the first pitch over for a strike then work the plate after that. But I was then a much better hitter when I had two strikes because I spread my stance to be able to wait on the ball longer and have a quick stroke.

My Time at Bat — A Story of Perseverance

You don't swing at bad pitches. You have to know that last strike is as important to you as it is to the pitcher. Don't give an inch, and know you will win the war.

When in the Minor Leagues, I didn't lose any sleep about who the pitcher was or what he threw. I knew I could see the ball and would hit it. In the big league, you can see it, but you're not going to hit it without doing your homework, for where you thought the pitch would be, it was not.

You must get the pitch you want or expect it to be in a certain spot. The pitcher knows if there is a weak spot, or certain pitchers you don't like or with whom you don't have a lot of success. He knows this because a team is scouted every game by different teams. They also know if you're hot or not. They know what pitch you like or don't like.

But what the scouting or meetings about you or your team can't control is your swinging the bat or what's in your mind about that pitcher. And if he doesn't get the ball in a certain spot, no report will help him. When a batter gets a certain pitch thrown where he is looking, he will not miss it often.

There are times when you have to make an adjustment when a pitcher keeps throwing you outside pitches and the umpire keeps calling strikes. It doesn't take a rocket scientist to know that you are too far from the plate.

When you hit well repeatedly, you are said to be in a zone. When this happens, every ball seems to be waiting for you to hit it as though it's on a tee. You see every pitch from the pitcher's hand very clearly, and it seems that almost every ball you hit finds a hold (base hit) or even a home run. The problem is that you only get into the zone *maybe* two or three times a year, and it doesn't last but two weeks at a time. There are only a few pitchers you face that no matter what they throw, you see the ball very well from his hand to the plate.

When it's the other way around, it is called a slump. The pitcher seems to be right on top of you, and you just don't pick the ball up as well as normal. Then if you hit a ball hard, it's always right to someone. That, too, can last for a couple of weeks. When you fall into this trap, you try to relax, focus and do what you can to get out of your slump as quickly as possible.

As you can see, there is so much one has to do to remain a good player day in and day out. Personally, I never kept a written log of what to look for

For Love of the Game

in certain situations—from pitcher to pitcher or from team to team. I would file things away in my mind, where no one but I knew where they were. I would retrieve them whenever I needed to. You never reveal your information. Because it works for you doesn't mean it will work for anyone else. It's the way you plan and study. You just keep your secrets and go about doing what you know will work for *you*. You take advice as it is needed. But deep down inside, you know what will work for you. You just add that advice to your body of information and adapt it to suit your needs.

This is primarily true of hitting. But it holds true in anything you do. You have to know what works for you. You should gather as much information and acquire as much knowledge as possible, but it is how you apply the knowledge that makes you wise. I always felt that no matter what, should I fail, it would be on my terms.

GETTING THE JOB DONE

There is so much growing up and learning that has to take place in your becoming a player who belongs in the Major League. Being able to hit, run, catch and throw is all I thought a baseball player needed to do. But I learned that a big part of the game is not only having talent and being able to think and relax, but also delivering. You must get the job done on and off the field, be a complete person, enjoy the people who you'll be with most of the time, be a person who loves what you do, and respect others for what they do. Think before you open your mouth about most things. After all, you don't want others to hurt you, so you should act the same way toward others.

There are rules and regulations that we all should follow, but you also must have a stop sign when it comes to doing anything that will hurt you, a team, another person, your family, your church or your God. Even being away from baseball for some time, I still learn that a person doesn't want to be around people who seem to have a chip on their shoulder or don't enjoy the simple things. Don't hog the conversation, listen to others, you will learn something.

No matter what, you must do whatever it takes to prepare yourself to get the job done when your time comes. There is nothing like being ready when it's your time. When you enjoy what you do and get rewarded for doing it well, you develop a hunger that often makes you want to do it all the time.

MY TIME AT BAT — A STORY OF PERSEVERANCE

That's the way it is supposed to work. Do your part to make the overall product the best. What a joy it is when things are going well, and being on a roll is so sweet.

It's no different in a game. You are part of a team that you help win games. It so happens that you are one of the few people to make it to the Major League, and if you are lucky, you get to stay some ten to twenty years. Prepare yourself to be one of the best on your job.

There are things you should be doing while you are waiting in the dugout to prepare yourself to perform your best. What you do may depend on when you are going to bat. You might go to the bathroom nearby. You might want to discuss the pitcher with someone. You could check out the pitcher for yourself. You also could encourage your teammates by telling them to get a hold of one.

What you really need to do, though, is stay in the game by watching and looking forward to your next at-bat. You might not be in the lineup that day, but you have to keep alert by knowing the count and being ready should you be called upon. Do you know what pitch was thrown, whether it was high or low, inside or outside, a strike or a ball? Did the hitter have a good swing, or did the pitcher really work him over, moving the ball around and getting him to swing at his pitch? The pitcher and batter face that every at-bat, pitch by pitch. If you don't get into their thinking, you are missing a lot of the game.

Did you notice that a pitcher acts a little differently when men are on base? You should be in the game enough to know why things happen. You should also think if a hit and run or a stolen base is in order.

In the dugout, you also should do a little stretching or loosen up. You had better stay wide awake when the batter is subject to hit the ball into the dugout. Many players have been hurt this way.

To be a Major Leaguer, you are expected to do what it takes to perform…period. No matter what. In everyday life, a person doesn't always feel good. At times, he has aches and pains. It is no different for a baseball player, even if he is in the best shape. There are days when you don't feel well; maybe a bruise or a cold with a fever will make you feel a little out of it. However, when the umpire says, "Play ball," that's what you must do. In most cases, you can shake it off and do your job. You have to realize that they expect you to perform. That's the bottom line. When you are hurting, it's

For Love of the Game

hard to concentrate. Yet on the field, you have to rise above it and give it your best. Sometimes you will have a good day even when you don't feel your best.

To remain in the league, you also are required to stay in shape or take a walk. Most teams check your weight every Sunday. The team wants you at a certain weight and sees that you stay very close to it. You will be fined if it is five pounds over. On the other hand, you are reminded if it's under too much. It doesn't matter if you are a regular or not, you have to stay in shape and be ready should you be called upon. A person who is not an everyday player still has to run every day to keep in shape plus complete his defensive work.

Many players have lost their positions because they did not keep themselves physically fit and because their mouths got them into trouble by complaining too much. It's a well-run business that pays you well, but to stay there, the bottom line is you must produce.

In my day, it also helped to stay in good shape because we played a lot of doubleheaders, which nowadays is rare. Whenever a game was rained out, it was scheduled as a doubleheader. Doubleheaders also were scheduled during most holidays.

IN THE CLUTCH

It can be more difficult to perform in clutch situations. I had to really work at keeping myself cool and focused in the clutch. It helped me to think that the pitcher was the one in trouble, not me. You have to want to be the one in that spot because you believe no one can do it better. Waiting on a good pitch and having a good swing every at-bat helps. That way, you aren't caught up in putting pressure on yourself.

I know I have at least three strikes, not one or two. You have to have patience at bat to make sure you don't help the pitcher by swinging at bad pitches. I've found that I enjoyed those times and was disappointed if I didn't get the job done. The same thing is true when you are on defense—you just want the ball to be hit to you because you know you will make the play. Those feelings don't come because you would like it to happen; they come with knowing that you have been there many times and have gotten the job done. I always felt I was the right man for the situation.

MY TIME AT BAT — A STORY OF PERSEVERANCE

There are times when you just have to deal with turning it up and believing you will get it done. It is called heart. Being able to stay cool and focused when the game is on the line is special, and only special people do it on a regular basis.

Whatever you have done that game is only good if you won. When you help to win a game with a catch, a bunt or another play, you feel like a king for a day.

However, being a big-leaguer, you are just as happy for a teammate who makes a good play that leads to a win. Pitching a no-hitter is special; a shutout is special; a game-ending catch or hit is special. In baseball, you know things such as the score of the game and what your hit would mean before you come to bat. I loved those times. I wanted in the worst way to be the one on whom the game rested. The winning hit is the one thing kids relate to. Well, to remain that kid was what I enjoyed. I never had a problem being focused, other than my first two at-bats in the Major League. My nerves let me down. I know for a fact many of my teammates couldn't get it done. But that was not the case with me. When it's clutch time, you have to be able to turn it up a notch.

GETTING READY FOR THE SEASON

Spring training plays a big part in preparing you to do your best in the upcoming season. While it doesn't take six weeks for an infielder, outfielder or catcher to get ready for a season, it does take pitchers that long because you can't rush their arms. They throw batting practice at first, then they work pick-off plays, then they throw on the side. When the exhibition season starts, pitchers will throw two, maybe three, innings and have a pitch count—meaning they will throw so many pitches. They will rest their arms a day or so, then throw on the side, always getting their running in because as a pitcher, your legs are as important as your arm. Pitchers will do this for five weeks until they work up to six or seven innings or a pitch count of at least 100.

Latin pitchers get bored because they have pitched during the winter league at home and are ready to go. In the first three weeks during batting practice, the Latin pitchers will be knocking the bat out of your hands. Their fastballs seem to be 200 miles an hour. Then when you catch up to them, it's

For Love of the Game

the other way around. You are ready now. Your hands are healing, or at least getting tough.

Your body is so sore from the exercise you do. Even when you hurt, you have to get your work in, including getting fly balls as an outfielder and ground balls as an infielder. Then you work on relays, which you will need to do when the ball is hit down the line or in between outfielders all the way to the fence. The infielder will come and line up the throw to him to be thrown to the base or home plate.

If the outfielder throws the ball low, sometimes it's hard to catch the ball. It makes everything hard to execute. Having a double cut-off man means that, depending on where the ball is hit, the shortstop will go first, then the second baseman will be his back-up and let him know where he should throw the ball. This is done when the batter has hit at least a double or triple. When the ball is hit to the left side of the outfield, the shortstop is the cut-off man, and the second baseman backs him up. The second baseman is the lead man when the ball is hit to the right side, with the shortstop the back-up.

A DAY AT WORK

On a typical game day in the Major League, at home, you report to the stadium at 4 P.M. for a 7:30 P.M. or 8 P.M. game. You put on your uniform and get ready for batting practice. You check to see if you are in the lineup, which is posted. Every player except the starting pitcher is on the field by 4:45 getting ready to shag for the players who are not in the lineup. They hit first for fifteen to twenty minutes. While the extra players are hitting, the players in the lineup are getting ground balls in the

1963

MY TIME AT BAT — A STORY OF PERSEVERANCE

infield and shagging fly balls in the outfield. This is also a good time to stretch your legs and do a little running to loosen up.

When the extra players finish hitting, those in the lineup hit for thirty minutes, while the extra players shag and take ground balls. The pitcher will run near the end of the batting practice. This is done every day at the same time, weather permitting.

Then you go to the clubhouse while the visiting team has batting practice. During this time, you sign at least three dozen balls that are put out by the clubhouse attendant. Then you change your underclothes because they are wet from your warming up. Then you go back to the dugout to get ready for infield practice. Some players throw with the same players every day; others loosen up with whoever is nearby. The home team takes the infield first for twenty minutes. After that they go change what needs to be changed–game shoes and maybe more under clothing and a clean uniform. You might eat a candy bar or a piece of fruit. The starting pitcher is now warming up, and you are getting ready by thinking over what you must do against that pitcher in all situations.

You get what you need as far as game equipment goes, and you even stop by the mirror to make sure everything is in place. Then you return to the dugout. This is when you might get to see the starting pitcher warming up. You and a few other players go loosen up some more by doing a couple of sprints. The lineups are being announced, and the managers or captains are at home plate exchanging the lineups.

Then the starting pitcher gives the sign that he is ready, and the players take the field for the national anthem. A game usually takes two to three hours. If you win, you congratulate those who did their part. When you lose, you remind one another that you will get them tomorrow. You unwind while you undress and hit the shower. Win or lose, you get ready to face the fans who will be waiting to get autographs. I always felt that this was my duty. I always gave fans my autograph because I knew they appreciated the kind of player I was, but mainly because I, too, wanted to be treated with respect. But you don't want to be surrounded by fans poking pencils, pens and paper in your face, seeking an autograph but not even opening their mouths to ask for one. I would tell them I would sign them all, but they had to line up. That worked out fine for me. Some of them had their kids with them.

For Love of the Game

Not only would fans be waiting for autographs after games, they would be waiting when you would go to your hotel. When you would go out to eat, they would be waiting in the hotel lobby or outside the hotel. They would be waiting when you would arrive at the stadium again after the game. It might be almost midnight by the time you can sign most of them. Fans don't understand that you are sometimes in a hurry because you have made plans maybe to have dinner with a couple of visiting players. But it doesn't matter what you have planned, you are a terrible person when you don't sign. For me, it was part of a day's work.

After you leave the stadium, you have dinner, go to bed and think about what you have to do and expect from the pitcher you might face the next day. On the road, things change just a little. You get a bus to the stadium, you check the time your team is supposed to hit, and you go from there. After a game on the road, you either take the bus back to your hotel or get a ride from a player from that city who will take you somewhere to eat. There are times on the road when you go to a relative or even a college teammate's home for dinner. This is the way I spent most of my days in the Major League.

We were given some Mondays off because of travel, as well as some Thursdays. But when you were rained out, those days were used for make-ups.

I loved being a Major League player. It was a dream come true. To fit in a win was part of a good day; a great day was when you won and did a good job at bat and in the field.

THAT LOSING FEELING

Losing didn't feel so good. An athlete works hard to keep from losing because it's not a good feeling any time at any level. A competitor never really learns to lose. Sure, out of respect, you congratulate the winner, but you have to deal with the hurt. At every level, you go over every little thing that you have to do to be the best you can be, but most of all, to win. You hear all the time how most guys work so hard on their game. The reason is not to be a loser.

My Time at Bat — A Story of Perseverance

Even when you have made a few defensive plays, but you lose the game, that feeling or bad taste is ever so present. Losing isn't taught anywhere. You understand that there will be a winner and a loser every game; you just don't ever want it to be you or your team. Winning, on the other hand, is always taught because everything you do is geared toward making you better to help your team be better, which figures into wins.

No one has to be taught to win or how to feel good. It's easy to get a pat on the back, or to be told you played a great game, had a big hit or made a great play. There are so many things that take place in a nine-inning baseball game, and many things could help win a game. That's why it's a must to be focused. You don't ever want to be the one who causes your team to lose.

A WINNING CAREER

But whether you win or lose a particular game, as a Major Leaguer, you have a winning career. You love going to work because you are not sure what each day is going to bring. You feel good about being a part of what is going on. There are so many things you have to do to maintain the level of competition you must face every day. You have to prove yourself on a regular basis. After all, you have to do more than just hit the ball and play defense. When at bat, you are all alone. In the field, you have to be ready to handle the hardest ball that can be hit to you. You have to know in advance what to do with the ball when it is hit to you. You could not imagine all the things you must do. But you do them. And you keep things in proper perspective.

1963

Epilogue

I'm very proud to have gotten so much love and to have learned to get along from my growing up in Rocky Mount. I am still in awe that I am the only black person from there to make it to the big league. It kind of blows my mind because so many black players were better than I was. I also know that being in the right place at the right time is so important. I know that God was on my side then and is more so now. No, it was not all peaches and cream, but I can sincerely say that every game for eleven years was special, and that's the way I played the game.

I've always thought the fans deserved to see your best effort because they paid, and getting to show them was so fun and thrilling for me. I just want to add that being a big-league baseball player for eleven years was everything I dreamed it would be. I never thought about the people you would meet in and out of baseball, the cities you would visit, the great shows, the best hotels, the best eating establishments, the best of everything. These were not what I ever envisioned. I only thought of what would take place on the field. The large crowds, the great teams, the best stadiums, the best baseball players in the world are what a player thinks about, along with, How will I do against the best? And will I fold under when the best I have to offer is being tested? As a player, there are other thoughts that cross your mind, but these are at the top of your mind.

For me, I knew I could play with any team and against any competition. This mindset is important in whatever you undertake in life. You first have to believe in your own ability, or you will not convince anyone else. There is no doubt that the very best players from all over the world are in the Major League. But surely, before you can get there, you have to prove you belong. You will pay your dues to get there; to stay, you will pay even more dues. It's a fact that many come and many go, but the ones who remain are there because they produce. As soon as your production goes down, see you later. You are judged on what you do, not what you might do. You might be a really good-looking player who can do it all during practice but little during games. You got it right, see you later. You know the team has many players in the Minor Leagues and even on the bench at the big-league level. You never think beyond the competition. At least I didn't.

You are a Major League player, and everyone expects you to do what a big-league player is supposed to do. This is not just during play. A player also is expected to be a swell person off the field. A Major League player has to carry himself with pride and dignity. It is the off-the-field things that could cause you not to be able to do your job on the field. There are so many people to whom you owe the opportunity of being in the Majors. You should not get yourself involved in anything that is not becoming because it reflects on your team and your family. You have to be in love with the Major League so you do not let anything interfere with your staying there. Being a complete baseball player is a wonderful thing, but being a complete human being is even better.

THE WINNING RUN

Baseball is a game that is supposed to bring you joy to play. The level of competition should never take the fun away. Winning makes things so much better, but whether you win or lose the game, you should have had fun and done all you could do to contribute.

Now, your part did not start during the game. Remember, you studied how the pitcher was going to pitch you and made other preparations for

Epilogue

being at bat or in the field. You respect the other team members, for they too are trying to win. And, of course, you understand that.

As in the game of baseball, I feel you should be ready in everyday life to do what you can to make things better and respect others. You go to bat every time you are around others. Make it your business to smile, speak and listen to them. Before you leave home, put on your smile and keep it on. Make everyone feel special. It will make you feel so much better. Life is about loving, sharing, caring and helping. And when you do those things, you will be filled with joy.

Signing autographs at a MLBPAA event. 1984

After all, people need people. To be happy, you should make others happy first. That is something I really learned in team sports. That's what rejoice means. We are all at bat all of the time. Don't wait for others; do your part. And always be ready when your opportunity knocks. You are the right person in the right spot. You can do it. Drive in the winning run. We are all pulling for you. Make us proud and happy. We all will rejoice! Congratulations and thank you for doing your part. I know you will do it.

THE TRUE MAJOR LEAGUER

I've enjoyed sharing highlights of my life with you. I hope you can use some of the principles I live by to shape your life. Seize the moment! Be prepared for whatever comes your way. Don't be afraid to share your talents. Be strong and courageous, and always believe in yourself. And don't forget to thank God; I did.

Too many players find out much too late that being a complete person is as important as being a good player. Many people realize that the amount

MY TIME AT BAT — A STORY OF PERSEVERANCE

of skill and talent it takes to be a Major League player is very little compared to being a nice person. It is not hard to treat people as you want to be treated. I am very proud to have been a Major League player, but I found it so pleasing to be a Major Person.

> *But seek ye first the kingdom of God, and his righteousness; and all these things shall be added unto you.* (Matthew 6:33)

Finally, I would like to leave this Scripture with you: 1 Corinthians 2:9. I want you to look it up. God loves you, and so do I!

–Chuck

Bunny and I, stronger than ever. 2002

CHUCK HINTON

Bats: Right **Throws:** Right
Height: 6' 1"
Weight: 180 lbs.
Born: May 3, 1934 in Rocky Mount, North Carolina

CAREER BATTING STATISTICS

YEAR	TEAM	AVG	G	AB	R	H	2B	3B	HR	RBI	BB	K	OBP	SLG	OPS
1961	Was	.260	106	339	51	88	13	5	6	34	40	81	.337	.381	.718
1962	Was	.310	151	542	73	168	25	6	17	75	47	66	.361	.472	.833
1963	Was	.269	150	566	80	152	20	12	15	55	64	79	.340	.426	.766
1964	Was	.274	138	514	71	141	25	7	11	53	57	77	.346	.414	.760
1965	Cle	.255	133	431	59	110	17	6	18	54	53	65	.336	.448	.784
1966	Cle	.256	123	348	46	89	9	3	12	50	35	66	.323	.402	.725
1967	Cle	.245	147	498	55	122	19	3	10	37	43	100	.304	.355	.659
1968	Cal	.195	116	267	28	52	10	3	7	23	24	61	.259	.333	.592
1969	Cle	.256	94	121	18	31	3	2	3	19	8	22	.303	.388	.691
1970	Cle	.318	107	195	24	62	4	0	9	29	25	34	.392	.477	.869
1971	Cle	.224	88	147	13	33	7	0	5	14	20	34	.317	.374	.691
Totals		.264	1353	3968	518	1048	152	47	113	443	416	685	.332	.412	.744

		BATTING						BASERUNNING			MISC	
YEAR	TEAM	HBP	GDP	TB	IBB	SH	SF	SB	CS	SB%	AB/HR	AB/K
1961	Was	1	5	129	1	0	3	22	5	.815	56.5	4.2
1962	Was	0	13	256	0	3	6	28	10	.737	31.9	8.2
1963	Was	1	14	241	2	8	7	25	9	.735	37.7	7.2
1964	Was	1	21	213	7	0	3	17	6	.739	46.7	6.7
1965	Cle	1	8	193	2	5	3	17	3	.850	23.9	6.6
1966	Cle	1	7	140	2	2	3	10	6	.625	29.0	5.3
1967	Cle	1	7	177	5	6	4	6	8	.429	49.8	5.0
1968	Cal	0	8	89	3	2	3	3	1	.750	38.1	4.4
1969	Cle	1	2	47	2	0	2	2	0	1.000	40.3	5.5
1970	Cle	0	3	93	1	2	2	0	2	.000	21.7	5.7
1971	Cle	0	3	55	2	0	0	0	0	--	29.4	4.3
Totals		7	91	1633	27	28	36	130	50	.722	35.1	5.8

Appearances on Leaderboards and Awards
Awards are **Year-League-Award**, Stats are **Year-Value-Rank**

All-Star	Batting Average	Triples	Stolen Bases
1964	1962 .310-4	1963 12-2	1961 22-4
		1964 7-7	1962 28-2
		1965 6-10	1963 25-2
			1964 17-5
			1965 17-7

FIELDING

YEAR	1961	1962	1962	1962	1963	1963	1963
TEAM	Was	Was	Was	Was	Was	Was	Was
POS	LF	LF	SS	2B	LF	SS	3B
G	92	136	1	12	125	2	19
PO	175	233	0	26	274	3	12
A	6	7	0	29	8	1	31
E	7	3	0	1	3	0	7
DP	4	1	0	15	1	0	5
FPCT	.963	.988	—	.982	.989	1.000	.860

YEAR	1963	1964	1964	1965	1965	1965	1965
TEAM	Was	Was	Was	Cle	Cle	Cle	Cle
POS	1B	LF	3B	LF	3B	2B	1B
G	6	131	2	72	1	23	40
PO	56	258	0	110	0	32	266
A	3	7	0	4	0	45	22
E	0	4	0	4	0	6	3
DP	3	3	0	0	0	9	21
FPCT	1.000	.985	—	.966	—	.928	.990

YEAR	1966	1966	1966	1967	1967	1968	1968
TEAM	Cle	Cle	Cle	Cle	Cle	Cal	Cal
POS	LF	2B	1B	LF	2B	LF	3B
G	104	2	6	136	5	37	13
PO	176	3	24	239	4	39	3
A	6	0	0	5	4	0	13
E	5	0	0	6	0	0	1
DP	1	0	2	0	2	0	0
FPCT	.973	1.000	1.000	.976	1.000	1.000	.941

FIELDING

YEAR	1968	1968	1969	1969	1970	1970	1970
TEAM	Cal	Cal	Cle	Cle	Cle	Cle	Cle
POS	2B	1B	LF	3B	LF	3B	2B
G	9	48	40	14	35	2	3
PO	14	334	32	5	36	1	0
A	14	33	0	15	4	0	1
E	1	5	2	1	1	0	0
DP	2	30	0	1	0	0	0
FPCT	.966	.987	.941	.952	.976	1.000	1.000

YEAR	1970	1970	1971	1971
TEAM	Cle	Cle	Cle	Cle
POS	1B	C	LF	1B
G	40	4	20	20
PO	164	28	18	83
A	8	2	0	5
E	1	0	0	0
DP	14	0	0	16
FPCT	.994	1.000	1.000	1.000

1971
Cle
C
5
22
0
0
0
1.000

TOTALS

G	1205
PO	2670
A	273
E	61
DP	130
FPCT	.980

Chuck Hinton Home Run Log

G=Game 1 or 2 of a double-header
DN=Day or Night Game
Bat=Batting Order
In=Inning
On=Men on base
PTeam=Pitching Team

HR#	Game Date	G	DN	Team	Pos	Bat	Pitcher	PTeam	Site	In	On	Out	Score Before HR	NOTES
1	05/21/1961 Sun	2	D	WAS	LF	3	Ron Kline	LAA	LAA	3	1	2	WAS: 1 LAA: 1	
2	05/27/1961 Sat		D	WAS	LF	3	Paul Giel	MIN	WAS	2	2	1	WAS: 5 MIN: 1	
3	06/09/1961 Fri	2	N	WAS	LF	3	Bob Shaw	CHA	WAS	2	1	1	WAS: 3 CHA: 0	
4	08/05/1961 Sat		D	WAS	RF	6	Juan Pizarro	CHA	CHA	7	0	0	WAS: 2 CHA: 3	
5	08/08/1961 Tue		N	WAS	RF	1	Barry Latman	CLE	CLE	5	0	0	WAS: 2 CLE: 0	
6	08/13/1961 Sun	1	D	WAS	LF	1	Bud Daley	NYA	WAS	1	0	0		Leadoff HR
7	04/20/1962 Fri		N	WAS	RF	1	Billy Hoeft	BAL	WAS	3	1	2	WAS: 0 BAL: 2	
8	06/01/1962 Fri		N	WAS	LF	5	Jim Donohue	MIN	MIN	12	0	1	WAS: 3 MIN: 3	
9	06/05/1962 Tue		N	WAS	LF	2	Milt Pappas	BAL	BAL	7	2	2	WAS: 2 BAL: 4	
10	06/07/1962 Thu		N	WAS	LF	2	Jack Fisher	BAL	BAL	3	1	0	WAS: 1 BAL: 6	
11	06/10/1962 Sun	2	D	WAS	LF	1	Jim Bunning	DET	WAS	1	0	0	WAS: 0 DET: 1	Leadoff HR
12	06/15/1962 Fri		N	WAS	LF	3	Milt Pappas	BAL	WAS	9	0	0	WAS: 2 BAL: 8	
13	06/16/1962 Sat		D	WAS	LF	3	Robin Roberts	BAL	WAS	1	0	2		
14	06/17/1962 Sun		D	WAS	LF	3	Hal Brown	BAL	WAS	4	0	0	WAS: 1 BAL: 3	
15	06/20/1962 Wed		D	WAS	LF	4	Don Mossi	DET	DET	7	1	2	WAS: 3 DET: 2	
16	06/21/1962 Thu		D	WAS	LF	4	Jim Bunning	DET	DET	4	0	1	WAS: 1 DET: 0	
17	06/29/1962 Fri		N	WAS	LF	6	Ray Moore	MIN	WAS	10	2	2	WAS: 3 MIN: 3	
18	07/06/1962 Fri		N	WAS	CF	5	Ed Rakow	KC	KC	4	0	0	WAS: 3 KC: 2	
19	07/22/1962 Sun	2	D	WAS	CF	5	Luis Arroyo	NYA	NYA	8	2	2	WAS: 4 NYA: 1	Inside-the-Park HR. 1st batter facing relief pitch
20	08/07/1962 Tue		N	WAS	RF	5	Bill Fischer	KC	WAS	9	1	1	WAS: 1 KC: 10	
21	08/09/1962 Thu		N	WAS	CF	3	Howie Koplitz	DET	WAS	7	1	2	WAS: 1 DET: 5	
22	08/23/1962 Thu	2	N	WAS	RF	3	Jim Kaat	MIN	MIN	5	0	1	WAS: 4 MIN: 0	
23	08/29/1962 Wed		N	WAS	2B	3	Chuck Estrada	BAL	WAS	8	1	2	WAS: 1 BAL: 8	Back-to-back HR (2)
24	04/22/1963 Mon		N	WAS	RF	3	Ken McBride	LAA	WAS	1	0	2		
25	04/23/1963 Tue		D	WAS	1B	3	Bo Belinsky	LAA	WAS	4	0	0		
26	04/27/1963 Sat		D	WAS	1B	5	John Wyatt	KC	WAS	8	0	2	WAS: 1 KC: 3	
27	04/29/1963 Mon	1	N	WAS	3B	4	Tom Morgan	LAA	LAA	9	1	2	WAS: 6 LAA: 3	
28	05/05/1963 Sun	2	D	WAS	3B	3	Hoyt Wilhelm	CHA	CHA	9	2	2	WAS: 5 CHA: 7	1st batter facing relief pitch

136

HR#	Game Date	G	DN	Team	Pos	Bat	Pitcher	PTeam	Site	In	On	Out	Score Before HR	NOTES
29	05/12/1963 Sun	1	D	WAS	3B	3	Earl Wilson	BOS	BOS	8	0	1	WAS: 1 BOS: 2	
30	05/12/1963 Sun	2	D	WAS	3B	3	Dave Morehead	BOS	BOS	1	0	2		
31	06/02/1963 Sun		D	WAS	LF	3	Dale Willis	KC	KC	10	1	1	WAS: 4 KC: 4	
32	06/09/1963 Sun		D	WAS	RF	3	Gary Bell	CLE	WAS	3	0	1	WAS: 1 CLE: 2	
33	07/13/1963 Sat		D	WAS	LF	4	Dick Hall	BAL	WAS	6	0	1	WAS: 3 BAL: 3	
34	07/15/1963 Mon		D	WAS	LF	3	Jim Bunning	DET	WAS	6	2	2	WAS: 5 DET: 3	
35	07/20/1963 Sat		D	WAS	RF	3	Dick Stigman	MIN	MIN	6	0	0	WAS: 1 MIN: 5	
36	08/06/1963 Tue	1	N	WAS	RF	3	Whitey Ford	NYA	WAS	1	0	2	WAS: 0 NYA: 2	Inside-the-Park
37	08/17/1963 Sat		D	WAS	RF	3	Bill Pleis	MIN	MIN	2	1	2	WAS: 5 MIN: 0	
38	08/26/1963 Mon	1	N	WAS	RF	3	Dick Stigman	MIN	WAS	6	1	2	WAS: 0 MIN: 2	
39	04/18/1964 Sat		D	WAS	LF	3	Dick Stigman	MIN	WAS	6	0	0	WAS: 3 MIN: 6	Back-to-back HR (2)
40	05/06/1964 Wed	1	N	WAS	LF	3	Jim Bouton	NYA	WAS	1	1	1		
41	05/06/1964 Wed	2	N	WAS	LF	3	Stan Williams	NYA	WAS	3	2	0	WAS: 0 NYA: 4	
42	05/09/1964 Sat		D	WAS	LF	3	Bob Heffner	BOS	WAS	7	0	1	WAS: 3 BOS: 4	
43	05/27/1964 Wed		D	WAS	LF	3	Bob Heffner	BOS	BOS	4	1	2	WAS: 5 BOS: 2	
44	05/31/1964 Sun	1	D	WAS	LF	3	Mudcat Grant	CLE	WAS	5	1	2	WAS: 3 CLE: 5	
45	06/07/1964 Sun	2	D	WAS	LF	3	Gary Bell	CLE	CLE	1	0	2		
46	07/05/1964 Sun	1	D	WAS	LF	4	Denny McLain	DET	DET	3	1	1	WAS: 2 DET: 2	
47	07/21/1964 Tue		N	WAS	LF	2	Jim Bouton	NYA	NYA	6	0	2	WAS: 0 NYA: 3	
48	07/28/1964 Tue		N	WAS	LF	3	Luis Tiant	CLE	WAS	5	2	2	WAS: 1 CLE: 2	
49	08/29/1964 Sat		D	WAS	LF	2	Johnny Klippstein	MIN	MIN	5	0	1	WAS: 3 MIN: 1	
50	04/30/1965 Fri		N	CLE	1B	2	Buster Narum	WAS	CLE	5	0	0	CLE: 2 WAS: 0	
51	05/01/1965 Sat		D	CLE	1B	2	Bennie Daniels	WAS	CLE	3	1	1	CLE: 0 WAS: 1	
52	05/15/1965 Sat		D	CLE	2B	7	Ron Kline	WAS	WAS	7	3	2	CLE: 2 WAS: 7	
53	05/21/1965 Fri		N	CLE	2B	7	Earl Wilson	BOS	CLE	4	0	0	CLE: 2 BOS: 2	
54	06/13/1965 Sun	2	D	CLE	LF	5	John O'Donoghue	KC	KC	2	0	0		
55	06/15/1965 Tue		N	CLE	1B	6	Steve Ridzik	WAS	CLE	5	0	2	CLE: 5 WAS: 2	
56	06/22/1965 Tue		N	CLE	LF	5	Al Worthington	MIN	MIN	10	0	0	CLE: 4 MIN: 4	
57	06/27/1965 Sun	1	D	CLE	1B	3	Jim Dickson	KC	CLE	15	2	2	CLE: 7 KC: 7	
58	07/19/1965 Mon		N	CLE	1B	5	Steve Barber	BAL	CLE	1	1	2	CLE: 1 BAL: 0	
59	07/20/1965 Tue		N	CLE	1B	5	Dave McNally	BAL	CLE	9	0	1	CLE: 0 BAL: 6	
60	07/21/1965 Wed	1	D	CLE	3B	5	Terry Fox	DET	DET	9	0	2	CLE: 4 DET: 10	
61	07/21/1965 Wed	2	N	CLE	CF	6	Denny McLain	DET	DET	2	0	0		
62	07/27/1965 Tue		N	CLE	CF	2	John Buzhardt	CHA	CHA	3	0	0	CLE: 2 CHA: 0	First AB of inning
63	07/30/1965 Fri		N	CLE	CF	2	Pedro Ramos	NYA	NYA	9	0	1	CLE: 2 NYA: 0	

HR#	Game Date	G	DN	Team	Pos	Bat	Pitcher	PTeam	Site	In	On	Out	Score Before HR	NOTES
64	08/14/1965 Sat		D	CLE	LF	3	Jim Kaat	MIN	CLE	5	0	2	CLE: 2 MIN: 1	
65	08/20/1965 Fri		N	CLE	LF	3	Buster Narum	WAS	WAS	4	0	0		
66	09/15/1965 Wed			CLE	CF	6	Dennis Bennett	BOS	BOS	8	2			
67	09/19/1965 Sun		D	CLE	CF	6	Juan Pizarro	CHA	CLE	4	0	2	CLE: 1 CHA: 5	
68	06/16/1966 Thu		N	CLE	PH	1	Steve Hamilton	NYA	NYA	9	2	2	CLE: 3 NYA: 7	Pinch hit for Vic Davalillo (CF)
69	07/05/1966 Tue		N	CLE	LF	2	Jim Merritt	MIN	CLE	3	0	2	CLE: 2 MIN: 1	
70	07/17/1966 Sun	1	D	CLE	CF	3	Hank Aguirre	DET	DET	3	0	0	CLE: 1 DET: 0	
71	07/17/1966 Sun	2	D	CLE	CF	3	Joe Sparma	DET	DET	3	2	1	CLE: 2 DET: 0	Back-to-back HR (1)
72	07/17/1966 Sun	2	D	CLE	CF	3	Orlando Pena	DET	DET	7	0	1	CLE: 10 DET: 0	Back-to-back HR (1)
73	07/19/1966 Tue		N	CLE	CF	3	Bruce Howard	CHA	CLE	1	1	1		
74	07/21/1966 Thu		N	CLE	CF	2	John Buzhardt	CHA	CLE	9	0	0	CLE: 0 CHA: 7	
75	07/22/1966 Fri		N	CLE	CF	3	Mickey Lolich	DET	CLE	7	2	2	CLE: 1 DET: 7	
76	08/06/1966 Sat		D	CLE	CF	3	Jim Bouton	NYA	CLE	6	1	1	CLE: 0 NYA: 1	
77	08/07/1966 Sun	2	D	CLE	LF	3	Al Downing	NYA	CLE	1	2	0	CLE: 0 NYA: 1	
78	08/15/1966 Mon		N	CLE	CF	3	Mike McCormick	WAS	CLE	5	1	1	CLE: 2 WAS: 1	
79	08/18/1966 Thu		N	CLE	CF	3	Gary Peters	CHA	CLE	7	0	2	CLE: 1 CHA: 0	
80	04/19/1967 Wed		D	CLE	RF	3	Bob Duliba	KC	CLE	8	0	1	CLE: 3 KC: 1	
81	04/21/1967 Fri		N	CLE	RF	3	Jack Sanford	CAL	CLE	3	0	1	CLE: 2 CAL: 0	Back-to-back HR (1)
82	05/20/1967 Sat		D	CLE	LF	2	Don McMahon	BOS	BOS	10	1	2	CLE: 3 BOS: 3	
83	05/22/1967 Mon		N	CLE	RF	3	Camilo Pascual	WAS	CLE	6	0	0	CLE: 3 WAS: 0	
84	06/13/1967 Tue	1	N	CLE	RF	2	George Brunet	CAL	CAL	8	0	1	CLE: 2 CAL: 8	
85	08/10/1967 Thu		N	CLE	RF	1	Dave McNally	BAL	CLE	1	0	0		Leadoff HR
86	08/24/1967 Thu		D	CLE	CF	1	Rickey Clark	CAL	CLE	4	0	0		
87	08/25/1967 Fri		N	CLE	RF	1	Jim Grant	MIN	CLE	1	0	0	CLE: 0 MIN: 1	Leadoff HR
88	08/28/1967 Mon	1	N	CLE	CF	1	Diego Segui	KC	KC	10	1	2	CLE: 4 KC: 4	
89	09/26/1967 Tue		D	CLE	LF	2	Jose Santiago	BOS	BOS	6	0	0	CLE: 3 BOS: 0	
90	04/11/1968 Thu		D	CAL	1B	4	Luis Tiant	CLE	CLE	7	0	1	CAL: 4 CLE: 5	
91	05/14/1968 Tue		N	CAL	1B	4	Gary Peters	CHA	CHA	7	0	2		Back-to-back HR (1)
92	05/15/1968 Wed		D	CAL	RF	5	Wilbur Wood	CHA	MIL	9	0	1	CAL: 3 CHA: 1	
93	05/25/1968 Sat		N	CAL	1B	5	Sam McDowell	CLE	CAL	5	2	2	CAL: 1 CLE: 0	
94	05/26/1968 Sun		D	CAL	2B	9	Luis Tiant	CLE	CAL	8	0	0	CAL: 1 CLE: 5	
95	07/11/1968 Thu		N	CAL	1B	4	Dick Ellsworth	BOS	CAL	7	0	0	CAL: 0 BOS: 2	
96	08/06/1968 Tue	1		CAL	3B	1	Frank Bertaina	WAS	WAS	1	0	0		Leadoff HR
97	07/04/1969 Fri	1	D	CLE	LF	5	Fritz Peterson	NYA	NYA	6	1	1		
98	07/27/1969 Sun		D	CLE	PH	9	Jerry Crider	MIN	CLE	8	1	1		Pinch hit for Stan Williams (P)

HR#	Game Date	G	DN	Team	Pos	Bat	Pitcher	PTeam	Site	In	On	Out	Score Before HR	NOTES
99	09/21/1969 Sun		D	CLE	PH	7	Darold Knowles	WAS	CLE	8	1	1		1st batter facing relief pitch
100	06/11/1970 Thu		N	CLE	PH	9	Marcel Lachemann	OAK	CLE	9	1	2	CLE: 2 OAK: 4	Pinch hit for Bob Miller (P). Stayed in game (RF)
101	06/21/1970 Sun	2	D	CLE	RF	7	Mike Kilkenny	DET	CLE	1	0	2	CLE: 4 DET: 1	
102	07/26/1970 Sun	1	D	CLE	RF	5	Bill Butler	KCA	CLE	4	0	0		
103	08/08/1970 Sat		D	CLE	PH	6	Darold Knowles	WAS	WAS	9	1	2	CLE: 2 WAS: 2	Pinch hit for Ted Uhlaender (RF)
104	08/30/1970 Sun		D	CLE	1B	5	Clyde Wright	CAL	CLE	3	0	2		
105	09/09/1970 Wed		N	CLE	1B	6	Joe Coleman	WAS	CLE	8	0	1		
106	09/11/1970 Fri		N	CLE	LF	4	Fritz Peterson	NYA	CLE	6	0	0		
107	09/26/1970 Sat		D	CLE	C	6	Jim Palmer	BAL	CLE	8	0	1	CLE: 0 BAL: 3	
108	09/27/1970 Sun		D	CLE	C	6	Jim Hardin	BAL	CLE	2	0	1		
109	05/23/1971 Sun	1	D	CLE	LF	6	Fritz Peterson	NYA	CLE	7	1	0	CLE: 1 NYA: 6	
110	06/20/1971 Sun	1	D	CLE	1B	9	Fred Scherman	DET	CLE	11	0	0	CLE: 6 DET: 6	
111	06/20/1971 Sun	2	D	CLE	C	6	Bill Zepp	DET	CLE	1	1	1	CLE: 3 DET: 1	
112	07/07/1971 Wed	2	N	CLE	C	6	Luis Tiant	BOS	CLE	1	2	2	CLE: 1 BOS: 0	
113	07/08/1971 Thu		N	CLE	C	7	Jim Lonborg	BOS	CLE	4	0	1	CLE: 2 BOS: 0	

Courtesy of David Vincent of the Society for American Baseball Research (SABR)

Homerun Report for Batter Chuck Hinton

Year	Team	Tot	XN	GS	LO	IP	PH	RHP	LHP
1961	WAS AL	6	0	0	1	0	0	4	2
1962	WAS AL	17	2	0	1	1	0	13	4
1963	WAS AL	15	1	0	0	1	0	10	5
1964	WAS AL	11	0	0	0	0	0	10	1
1965	CLE AL	18	2	1	0	0	0	12	6
1966	CLE AL	12	0	0	0	0	1	5	7
1967	CLE AL	10	2	0	2	0	0	8	2
1968	CAL AL	7	0	0	1	0	0	2	5
1969	CLE AL	3	0	0	0	0	2	1	2
1970	CLE AL	9	0	0	0	0	2	4	5
1971	CLE AL	5	1	0	0	0	0	3	2
TOTAL		113	8	1	5	2	5	72	41

Chuck Hinton Homerun Facts

Rank among batters: 517 of 6,367

HR in both Gm of doubleheader - @ BOS: 05/12/1963; vs NYA: 05/06/1964; @ DET: 07/21/1965; @ DET: 07/17/1966; vs DET: 06/20/1971

Career Home Run #1: hit for WAS (AL) on
   05/21/1961 vs. Ron Kline (RHP) of LAA at LAA
   Game #2 Inning: 3 Men On Base: 1
   It was a day game and he was 27.018 years.days old.

Career Home Run #100: hit for CLE (AL) on
   06/11/1970 vs. Marcel Lachemann (RHP) of OAK at CLE
       Inning: 9 Men On Base: 1
   It was a night game and he was 36.039 years.days old.

Career Home Run #113: hit for CLE (AL) on
   07/08/1971 vs. Jim Lonborg (RHP) of BOS at CLE
       Inning: 4 Men On Base: 0
   It was a night game and he was 37.066 years.days old.

88 Pitchers Surrendered Home Runs
The Top 10

Total	Name	Total	Name
4	Luis Tiant (RHP)	2	Gary Bell (RHP)
3	Jim Bunning (RHP) (HOF)	2	Bob Heffner (RHP)
3	Dick Stigman (LHP)	2	Mudcat Grant (RHP)
3	Jim Bouton (RHP)	2	Denny McLain (RHP)
3	Fritz Peterson (LHP)	2	Buster Narum (RHP)
2	Ron Kline (RHP)	2	Dave McNally (LHP)
2	Juan Pizarro (LHP)	2	John Buzhardt (RHP)
2	Milt Pappas (RHP)	2	Gary Peters (LHP)
2	Jim Kaat (LHP)	2	Darold Knowles (LHP)
2	Earl Wilson (RHP)		

Teams Surrendering Home Runs

15 DET AL (13.3%)
14 MIN AL (12.4%)
13 NYA AL (11.5%)
13 BAL AL (11.5%)
11 BOS AL (9.7%)
11 WAS AL (9.7%)
10 CHA AL (8.8%)
8 CLE AL (7.1%)
8 KC AL (7.1%)
4 LAA AL (3.5%)
4 CAL AL (3.5%)
1 OAK AL (0.9%)
1 KCA AL (0.9%)

Home Runs by Cities

43 CLE AL (38.1%)
30 WAS AL (26.5%)
8 DET AL (7.1%)
6 BOS AL (5.3%)
5 MIN AL (4.4%)
5 NYA AL (4.4%)
4 KC AL (3.5%)
4 CAL AL (3.5%)
3 CHA AL (2.7%)
2 LAA AL (1.8%)
2 BAL AL (1.8%)
1 MIL AL (0.9%)

Ballparks Homered In
In Order "Conquered"

HRs	Ballparks	HRs	Ballparks
1	Wrigley Field (Los Angeles, CA)	8	Tiger Stadium (Detroit, MI)
3	Griffith Stadium (Washington, DC)	4	Municipal Stadium (Kansas City, MO)
3	Comiskey Park I (Chicago, IL)	5	Yankee Stadium (New York, NY)
43	Cleveland Stadium (Cleveland, OH)	1	Dodger Stadium (Los Angeles, CA)
27	Robert F. Kennedy Stadium (Washington, DC)	6	Fenway Park (Boston, MA)
5	Metropolitan Stadium (Minneapolis, MN)	4	Anaheim Stadium (Anaheim, CA)
2	Memorial Stadium (Baltimore, MD)	1	County Stadium (Milwaukee, WI)

Total ballparks = 14

Pitcher Alphabetical Listing

Total	Name	Total	Name
1	Hank Aguirre (LHP)	1	Jim Lonborg (RHP)
1	Luis Arroyo (LHP)	1	Ken McBride (RHP)
1	Steve Barber (LHP)	1	Mike McCormick (LHP)
1	Bo Belinsky (LHP)	1	Sam McDowell (LHP)
2	Gary Bell (RHP)	2	Denny McLain (RHP)
1	Dennis Bennett (LHP)	1	Don McMahon (RHP)
1	Frank Bertaina (LHP)	2	Dave McNally (LHP)
3	Jim Bouton (RHP)	1	Jim Merritt (LHP)
1	Hal Brown (RHP)	1	Ray Moore (RHP)
1	George Brunet (LHP)	1	Dave Morehead (RHP)
3	Jim Bunning (RHP) (HOF)	1	Tom Morgan (RHP)
1	Bill Butler (LHP)	1	Don Mossi (LHP)
2	John Buzhardt (RHP)	2	Buster Narum (RHP)
1	Rickey Clark (RHP)	1	John O'Donoghue (LHP)
1	Joe Coleman (RHP)	1	Jim Palmer (RHP) (HOF)
1	Jerry Crider (RHP)	2	Milt Pappas (RHP)
1	Bud Daley (LHP)	1	Camilo Pascual (RHP)
1	Bennie Daniels (RHP)	1	Orlando Pena (RHP)
1	Jim Dickson (RHP)	2	Gary Peters (LHP)
1	Jim Donohue (RHP)	3	Fritz Peterson (LHP)
1	Al Downing (LHP)	2	Juan Pizarro (LHP)
1	Bob Duliba (RHP)	1	Bill Pleis (LHP)
1	Dick Ellsworth (LHP)	1	Ed Rakow (RHP)
1	Chuck Estrada (RHP)	1	Pedro Ramos (RHP)
1	Bill Fischer (RHP)	1	Steve Ridzik (RHP)
1	Jack Fisher (RHP)	1	Robin Roberts (RHP) (HOF)
1	Whitey Ford (LHP) (HOF)	1	Jack Sanford (RHP)
1	Terry Fox (RHP)	1	Jose Santiago (RHP)
1	Paul Giel (RHP)	1	Fred Scherman (LHP)
2	Mudcat Grant (RHP)	1	Diego Segui (RHP)
1	Dick Hall (RHP)	1	Bob Shaw (RHP)
1	Steve Hamilton (LHP)	1	Joe Sparma (RHP)
1	Jim Hardin (RHP)	3	Dick Stigman (LHP)
2	Bob Heffner (RHP)	4	Luis Tiant (RHP)
1	Billy Hoeft (LHP)	1	Hoyt Wilhelm (RHP) (HOF)
1	Bruce Howard (RHP)	1	Stan Williams (RHP)
2	Jim Kaat (LHP)	1	Dale Willis (RHP)
1	Mike Kilkenny (LHP)	2	Earl Wilson (RHP)
2	Ron Kline (RHP)	1	Wilbur Wood (LHP)
1	Johnny Klippstein (RHP)	1	Al Worthington (RHP)
2	Darold Knowles (LHP)	1	Clyde Wright (LHP)
1	Howie Koplitz (RHP)	1	John Wyatt (RHP)
1	Marcel Lachemann (RHP)	1	Bill Zepp (RHP)
1	Barry Latman (RHP)		
1	Mickey Lolich (LHP)		Total Hall of Famers on list: 5

Home Runs vs. Right- and Left-Handed Pitchers

vs. right: 72 (63.7%)
vs. left: 41 (36.3%)

Home Runs by Day of Week

Sun	30	(26.5%)
Mon	8	(7.1%)
Tue	17	(15.0%)
Wed	12	(10.6%)
Thu	13	(11.5%)
Fri	15	(13.3%)
Sat	18	(15.9%)

Home Runs by Month

Apr	10	(8.8%)
May	20	(17.7%)
Jun	24	(21.2%)
Jul	27	(23.9%)
Aug	24	(21.2%)
Sep	8	(7.1%)
Oct	0	(0.0%)

Home Runs by Defensive Position

C	5
1B	15
2B	4
3B	6
LF	39
CF	19
RF	20
PH	5

Home Runs by Innings & Men On Base

	Men On Base					
Inn	0	1	2	3	Unk	Totals
1	11	4	2	0	0	17 (15.0%)
2	3	3	0	0	0	6 (5.3%)
3	5	6	2	0	0	13 (11.5%)
4	10	1	0	0	0	11 (9.7%)
5	6	2	2	0	0	10 (8.8%)
6	7	3	1	0	0	11 (9.7%)
7	7	3	2	1	0	13 (11.5%)
8	7	3	2	0	0	12 (10.6%)
9	6	4	2	0	0	12 (10.6%)
10	1	3	1	0	0	5 (4.4%)
11	1	0	0	0	0	1 (0.9%)
12	1	0	0	0	0	1 (0.9%)
15	0	0	1	0	0	1 (0.9%)
Tot	65	32	15	1	0	113
Pct	57.5	28.3	13.3	0.9	0.0	

Courtesy of David Vincent of the Society for American Baseball Research (SABR)

Become An Alumni Member
Your Ticket to the Big Leagues

You have shivered with anticipation as your team trotted out to take the field. Screamed yourself hoarse in the stands. Held your breath right along with the batter as the game came down to a single pitch, a single swing. You have also been a part of the "Swing with the Legends" Golf Series. **Here is your chance to keep in touch with Alumni members.**

By joining the MLBPAA you will be part of an organization dedicated to perpetuating the game of baseball. As a member you not only advance the game of baseball but you also provide the Association the opportunity to accomplish more important goals, like helping our youth.

Youth has become a major focus for the Alumni. They are our future. Our program, "Legends for Youth" is a series of free baseball clinics run by the MLBPAA. It exists to inspire today's youth through positive sports images. Besides teaching the basics, we stress the need for goals, the avoidance of drugs and the importance of education. We feel this program is so important that **$10 of your membership** dues goes directly into supporting these **free baseball clinics**.

Now is your chance to make a difference. Join today! Together, we can keep the game of baseball alive and well for players and fans of today and tomorrow.

This Space Available.

Join more than 5000 Major Leaguers and baseball fans who support the MLBPAA "Legends for Youth" programs.

TO JOIN CALL:
800-336-5272
postoffice@mlbpaa.com
www.baseball-legends.com

Membership Includes:
- *Baseball Alumni News* Subscription
- Authentic Membership Certificate
- Official Alumni Merchandise
- And More…

MAJOR LEAGUE BASEBALL ®
PLAYERS ALUMNI

For additional copies of this book,
contact your local bookstore
or the distributor listed below.

Chuck@Mytimeatbat.com

1933 Whitfield Park Loop · Sarasota, Florida 34243
(800) 444-2524 · FAX (800) 777-2525
www.bookworld.com

To have this book autographed, please send your book, a money order made payable to "Charles Hinton," and a self-addressed, stamped mailer (at least $4 postage should be affixed) to the author at the address below:

Author Contact

Chuck Hinton
6330 16th Street, N.W.
Washington, D.C. 20011

Please visit **http://www.MyTimeAtBat.com** to leave feedback about the book, for additional information and products available from Chuck Hinton, to order more copies, and much more...

Additional Product by Chuck Hinton
VIDEO *Hitting—Keep It Simple*

Chuck Hinton, veteran Major League Player, baseball and softball coach, illustrates hitting and the tried and true aspects of the craft you've never imagined. He reveals the secrets to successful split-second decisions and adjustments in the batter's box.

Hitting—Keep It Simple principles, presented in a simple and effective way, can be gleaned by any aspiring baseball player, from Little League to the Major Leagues. It is also a great coaching tool!

Chuck Hinton will teach you:

- The correct swing
- The correct stance
- The correct stride
- The correct focus
- The correct practice
- The correct results

"Done correctly, you can't miss." — Chuck Hinton

Hitting—Keep It Simple VIDEO

VHS
NTSC format (US and Canada only)
Color
60 minutes
ISBN 1-56229-004-5
UPC 78011200633
$19.99

To order
Call BookWorld at 1-800-444-2524
or
Visit www.MyTimeAtBat.com